Immigration and
School Safety

Immigration and School Safety utilizes a multidisciplinary approach to expose the complex relationship between immigration and school safety in the United States. It addresses not only individual, intrapersonal, and environmental factors but also distant-level conditions that are relevant to the experiences of immigrant children and connected to school safety. Twenty-five percent of all youth in U.S. schools have at least one immigrant parent, and that percentage is expected to increase to 33 percent by 2040.

A wide array of factors, including but not limited to laws, public and political discourses, educational policies, interpersonal relationships, socioeconomic status, English language proficiency, citizenship, legal status, family characteristics, race and ethnicity, generational status, nationality, religion, and gender, contribute to the marginalizing experiences of children of immigrants at school. With the rapid growth of students in immigrant families in U.S. schools, any effort to address school violence and implement school safety policies must consider barriers associated with the unique educational experiences of that segment. This book highlights the often overlooked importance of immigration as a mediating factor in explaining both violence and victimization and provides a blueprint for integrating immigration and criminology theories into evidence-based efforts toward ensuring safety for all students.

The authors demonstrate that immigration matters significantly in school violence and safety concerns and illustrate why research that integrates immigration with criminology theories is needed to understand the causes and correlates of school violence. The book will appeal to a wide array of individuals, including academics, educators, policymakers, practitioners, social workers, parents, and stakeholders who are committed to addressing educational disparities and inequities associated with immigration and school safety.

Dr. Anthony A. Peguero is Professor in the School of Criminology and Criminal Justice and the T. Denny Sanford School of Social and Family Dynamics at Arizona State University. Dr. Peguero's research focuses on youth violence, socialization and marginalization, education, and the adaptation of the children of immigrants. Overarching themes in Dr. Peguero's research include the barriers and challenges faced by the children of immigrants; how social inequality is central to sociological and criminological theories toward understanding and addressing youth violence; the intersection of race/ethnicity, immigration, and gender in relationship to youth marginalization, particularly within schools; and policies intended to promote safety and equity for youth. Dr. Peguero serves as the Director of the Laboratory for the Study of Youth Inequality and Justice, Research Fellow at the Institute for Society, Culture and Environment, and Research Affiliate of the Center for Peace Studies and Violence Prevention at Virginia Tech. He is also a member of the Racial Democracy, Crime, and Justice Network and co-founder of Latina/o/x Criminology, which both hold the goals of advancing research on the intersection of race, crime, and justice and promoting racial democracy within the study of these issues by supporting junior scholars from underrepresented groups.

Dr. Jennifer M. Bondy is Associate Professor in the School of Social Transformation at Arizona State University. Her research focuses on three interrelated lines of inquiry: 1) Latina youth citizenship formations, 2) school socialization of the children of immigrants, and 3) the intersections of teacher education and documentation status. Dr. Bondy is Co-Director of the Laboratory for the Study of Youth Inequality and Justice. She also serves as Co-Chair for Division K: Teaching and Teacher Education, Section IV: Marginality, Equity, and Justice in PK–16 settings for the American Educational Research Association. Dr. Bondy is currently an editorial board member for the *American Educational Research Journal*; *Race, Ethnicity and Education*; *Taboo: The Journal of Culture and Education*; and the *Journal of Curriculum and Pedagogy*. Prior to becoming an academic, Dr. Bondy taught high school for four years.

Crime and Society Series
Edited by Hazel Croall
University of Glasgow

For more information about this series, please visit: www.routledge.com

Immigration and School Safety

Anthony A. Peguero and
Jennifer M. Bondy

Routledge
Taylor & Francis Group

NEW YORK AND LONDON

First published 2021
by Routledge
52 Vanderbilt Avenue, New York, NY 10017

and by Routledge
2 Park Square, Milton Park, Abingdon, Oxon, OX14 4RN

Routledge is an imprint of the Taylor & Francis Group, an informa business

Library of Congress Cataloging-in-Publication Data
A catalog record for this book has been requested

ISBN: 978-0-367-35691-0 (hbk)
ISBN: 978-0-367-74118-1 (pbk)
ISBN: 978-0-429-34139-7 (ebk)

Typeset in Bembo
by Apex CoVantage, LLC

To the children of immigrants who endure violence, persevere in the face of adversity, and overcome obstacles in their pursuit to achieve success and represent their families, communities, and themselves.

To the educators, policymakers, and community stakeholders who are welcoming and committed to facilitating the well-being of immigrants and their children.

We stand with you.

Contents

Preface

It is well established that schools are primary agents of socialization. After one's own family, school is often the first place a child learns society's norms, values, and culture and comes to understand his or her roles and responsibilities in society, as well as civic orientations and engagement. Thus, violence and disorder occurring within schools has received increased attention and scrutiny over the years because schools are contexts of socialization that directly influence youth development, educational progress, and life-course trajectories. Although for the most part schools in the United States are safe places for students, it is also evident that disorder, violence, and victimization rates are not equally occurring across schools. Simultaneously, vulnerable and marginalized youth are often most likely to attend disadvantaged and disorderly schools, face educational hurdles and barriers, be victimized, and be disproportionately surveilled and punished. There is some question, however, if a "one-size-fits-all" approach toward making schools safe can be fully realized without considering the distinct vulnerabilities that the children of immigrants face in schools. With the evident rapid growth of students in immigrant families in the U.S. educational system, any effort to address school violence and implementation of school safety policies must consider barriers and hurdles associated with the children of immigrants' schooling and educational experiences. In this book, we present and depict the significance of immigration in efforts to address school violence while also ensuring safe learning environments.

Acknowledgments

Gratitude is extended for the helpful comments and constructive suggestions from Ellen Boyne, editor of this book series, for her steadfast encouragement, support, and patience, as well as to everyone at Routledge and the blind reviewers throughout the development of this book. Appreciation is conveyed for the support offered by the Racial Democracy, Crime and Justice Network and Latina/o/x Criminology. This research was in part supported by the National Institute of Justice (Grant#2012-NIJ-CX-0003) and National Science Foundation (Grant#2016-NSF-SES-1625703). Additional research support was also provided by the Institute for Society, Culture and Environment and the Center for Peace Studies and Violence Prevention at Virginia Tech. The perspectives, findings, views, conclusions, and recommendations expressed in this book are those of the authors and do not necessarily reflect and should not be attributed to any of the funders or supporting organizations mentioned herein.

Anthony A. Peguero: I would like to thank Ellen Boyne for the opportunity to publish this book and her editorship. I would like to thank my co-author, Dr. Jennifer M. Bondy, for our collaboration on this book. We have collaborated with each other for decades, and it has been a great learning experience and privilege to work along with her throughout this process. On a more personal note, I would like to thank all the mentors, students, mentees, colleagues, friends, and family who have been supportive throughout this research enterprise. I incredibly appreciate our home with a loving, supportive, adventurous, and patient partner, as well as wonderful and playful dogs who all remind me of the daily importance of love and laughter in life. I try my best to represent all of you with my scholarship and academic pursuits. Finally, as a child of an Ecuadorian immigrant mother and Dominican immigrant father, I acknowledge all the children of immigrants who are facing, enduring, persisting against, and overcoming the challenges, hurdles, and trauma of attending unsafe school environments. Ultimately, the children of immigrants are the bedrock of the United States' academic and economic future.

Jennifer M. Bondy: This book would not have been possible without the support and encouragement of many people. I thank Ellen Boyne for remaining a helpful editor throughout this process and for making the manuscript the best that it could be. For their integrity, leadership, and generosity in protecting my time as an assistant professor when this book was first started, I thank Sharon Johnson and John Ryan. Affection and numerous conversations over the years with a number of individuals have indelibly shaped my thinking. I have learned much from Brent J. Johnson, Lauren Braunstein, and Takumi Sato. To the preservice teachers whom I taught years ago, thank you for sharing your passion to educate all children well. My hope is that this book addresses silences in teacher education and ameliorates the educational marginalization of the children of immigrants. My family has also sustained me in their own unique ways – my parents, Yvonne and Peter; my sister, Julie; my brother, Peter; my aunt, Brenda, whom we called Nan and who is no longer with us; my cousins, Bella, Adriana, and Humberto; and my aunt, Bella. Last, but certainly not least, I thank my friend and co-author, Dr. Anthony A. Peguero. We have been collaborating for a number of years. I have benefited greatly from his insights and comments, and he remains my most ardent supporter. And, of course, I thank our dogs, Nana, Quito, and Nola. Nana unexpectedly departed from this world last year, but she, Quito, and Nola have brought indescribable joy and affection into our family and home. They, too, sustain and comfort me in their own ways.

Chapter 1

Introduction

It is well established that schools are primary agents of socialization. After one's own family, the school is often the first place a child learns society's norms, values, and culture and comes to understand his or her roles and responsibilities in society, as well as civic orientations and engagement (Gottfredson, 2001; Kupchik, 2010, 2016; Rios, 2011, 2017; Shedd, 2015). John Dewey (1916) first called attention to the link between education and democracy, arguing that public schools could level the playing field between the advantaged and the less advantaged, and serve as apprenticeships for civic life. Since Dewey's seminal work, and given the powerful socializing effect of schools, researchers have scrutinized the socialization processes that occur in schools, recognizing the long-lasting and far-reaching impact schools may have. Thus, violence and disorder occurring within schools have received increased attention and scrutiny over the years because schools are contexts of socialization that directly influence youth development, educational progress, and life-course trajectories (Gottfredson, 2001; Kupchik, 2010, 2016; Morris, 2016; Rios, 2011, 2017; Shedd, 2015). Moreover, in the aftermath of fatal mass shootings at Columbine High School, Virginia Tech, and Sandy Hook Elementary School, social, cultural, political, and justice responses toward ensuring healthy and safe learning environments have only heightened expectations to address violence and disorder within schools (Muschert & Peguero, 2010; Muschert, Henry, Bracy, & Peguero, 2013; Schildkraut & Muschert, 2019; Tanner-Smith, Fisher, Addington, & Gardella, 2018). Although for the most part, schools in the United States are safe places for students, it is also evident that disorder, violence, and victimization rates are not equally occurring across schools, as well as distinct segments of the student population (Musu et al., 2019). Simultaneously, vulnerable and marginalized youth are often most likely to attend disadvantaged and disorderly schools, face educational hurdles and barriers, be victimized, and be disproportionately surveilled and punished (Durán, 2013, 2018; Morris, 2016; Noguera, 2009; Rios, 2011, 2017; Shedd, 2015). There is some question, however, if a "one-size-fits-all" approach toward making schools safe can be fully realized without considering the distinct vulnerabilities that the children of immigrants face in the U.S. school system.

Approximately 43 million residents, or 13 percent of the total U.S. population, are foreign-born. Twenty-five percent of all youth in American schools have at least one immigrant parent and that percentage is expected to increase to 33 by 2040 (U.S. Census Bureau, 2017). According to the U.S. Department of Education (2015), there are approximately 840,000 immigrant students and more than 4.6 million English language learners in the U.S. educational system. A wide array of factors, such as laws, public and political discourses, educational policies, interpersonal relationships, socioeconomic status, English language proficiency, citizenship, legal status, family characteristics, race and ethnicity, generational status, nationality, religion, and gender contribute to disparate and marginalizing experiences the children of immigrants endure at school (Bondy, 2015, 2016; Gonzales, 2016; Hong, Merrin, Peguero, Gonzalez-Prendes, & Lee, 2016; Peguero, 2009, 2011, 2012a, 2012b, 2013; Peguero & Bondy, 2011, 2015; Peguero & Hong, 2019; Portes & Rumbaut, 2014; Kao, Vaquera, & Goyette, 2013). Thus, with the evident rapid growth of students in immigrant families in American schools, any effort to address school violence and implement school safety policies must consider barriers and hurdles associated with the children of immigrants' schooling and educational experiences.

In general, we present and depict the significance of immigration matters in future efforts to address school violence while also ensuring safe learning environments. Our second chapter discusses in further detail how immigration matters with regard to school violence and safety. In this second chapter, we provide the definition of and perspectives about school violence and safety that are incorporated in our book. We also discuss the significance of the context of reception for immigrants and their children. We then highlight the complexities and details surrounding the "immigrant criminal" myth, as well as how it matters toward violence and safety for immigrants and their children, as well as the dilemma of the "school to prison/deportation pipeline." Next, we highlight the significance of the social, political, and educational climate around immigration and how it impacts school safety. We then conclude this second chapter by explaining theories of assimilation, such as straight-line, segmented, and immigrant optimism, to demonstrate their relevance within schools.

In the third chapter, the intersecting factors associated with immigration and school safety are presented. As we demonstrate, exposure to violence and victimization at school is disparate across distinct segments of the student population, especially for the children of immigrants. However, it is also evident that the population of children of immigrants attending U.S. schools is also diverse. There are further inequalities associated with the population of children of immigrants in terms of their school safety. We review the relevance of the intersection of factors, such as race, ethnicity, region of origin, gender, English language proficiency, family, and documentation status in association with school violence and safety.

In the fourth chapter, we argue why further research that incorporates and integrates immigration with criminology theories is needed to understand the causes and correlates of school violence. In this chapter, we state that it is imperative for researchers, policymakers, and community stakeholders who are pursuing evidence-based efforts toward ensuring safety for all students to utilize criminology theories in order to understand the relationships between immigration and school safety. We also demonstrate that there is a school violence "immigrant paradox" occurring within U.S. schools that warrants discussion. This paradox has also fueled criminological investigation; however, only a limited number of studies have investigated the role of immigration in understanding and addressing school violence, as well as ensuring safety for the children of immigrants. We highlight five theoretical approaches that are often utilized to address school violence and pursue safety for students: 1) social-ecology, 2) social bonds, 3) opportunity, 4) minority threat, and 5) procedural justice. We also underscore research evidence that clearly suggests immigration is important to consider within the tenets of these theories. We summarize research findings that denote how the utilization of these theories can explain the children of immigrants' engagement in offending, highlight vulnerability to violence and victimization, ensure safety, and improve educational experiences; however, the need to further integrate immigration and criminology theories toward future research about school safety is warranted.

In the fifth chapter, we discuss policy implications and the importance of addressing the complexities associated with immigration when considering the safety of the nation's fastest-growing segment of the student population – the children of immigrants. We present the policy implications for school personnel, as well as programmatic

Introduction

approaches toward addressing violence and ensuring safety. We highlight how school safety policies (i.e., zero-tolerance and social control,
school-wide positive behavioral interventions and support programs,
communal schools, Olweus bullying prevention programs, and restorative justice) should consider factors associated with immigration.
We then conclude by summarizing and highlighting the importance
of appreciating the symbiotic relationships between educational success, progress, and well-being when pursuing safe healthy learning
environments, especially for marginalized youth, such as the children
of immigrants. We emphasize the takeaways associated with *Immigration and School Safety* and the complexities associated with immigration
and safety, as well as the need for further research.

References

Bondy, J. M. (2015). Hybrid citizenship: Latina youth and the politics of belonging. *The High School Journal, 98*(4), 353–373.
Bondy, J. M. (2016). Latina youth, education, and citizenship: A feminist transnational analysis. *Theory & Research in Social Education, 44*(2), 212–243.
Dewey, J. (1916). *Democracy and education: An introduction to the philosophy of educa-
tion.* New York: Palgrave Macmillan.
Durán, R. J. (2013). *Gang life in two cities: An insider's journey.* New York: Colum-
bia University Press.
Durán, R. J. (2018). *The gang paradox: Inequalities and miracles on the U.S.-Mexico
border.* New York: Columbia University Press.
Gonzales, R. G. (2016). *Lives in limbo: Undocumented and coming of age in America.*
Berkeley, CA: University of California Press.
Gottfredson, D. C. (2001). *Schools and delinquency.* New York: Cambridge Uni-
versity Press.
Hong, J. S., Merrin, G. J., Peguero, A. A., Gonzalez-Prendes, A. A., & Lee, N.
Y. (2016). Exploring the social-ecological determinants of physical fighting in
U.S. schools: What about youth in immigrant families? *Child & Youth Care
Forum, 45*(2), 279–299.
Kao, G., Vaquera, E., & Goyette, K. (2013). *Education and immigration.* Malden,
MA: Policy Press.
Kupchik, A. (2010). *Homeroom security: School discipline in an age of fear.* New York:
New York University Press.
Kupchik, A. (2016). *The real school safety problem: The long-term consequences of harsh
school punishment.* Oakland: University of California Press.
Morris, M. W. (2016). *Pushout: The criminalization of Black girls in schools.* New
York: The New Press.
Muschert, G. W., Henry, S., Bracy, N. L., & Peguero, A. A. (2013). *Responses to
school violence: Confronting the Columbine effect.* Boulder, CO: Lynne Reinner
Publishers.

Muschert, G. W., & Peguero, A. A. (2010). The Columbine effect and school anti-violence policy. *Research in Social Problems & Public Policy, 17*, 117–148.

Musu, L., Zhang, A., Wang, K., Zhang, J., & Oudekerk, B.A. (2019). *Indicators of School Crime and Safety: 2018* (NCES 2019-047/NCJ 252571). Washington, DC: National Center for Education Statistics, U.S. Department of Education, and Bureau of Justice Statistics, Office of Justice Programs, U.S. Department of Justice.

Noguera, P. A. (2009). *The trouble with Black boys: And other reflections on race, equity, and the future of public education.* San Francisco, CA: Jossey-Bass.

Peguero, A. A. (2009). Victimizing the children of immigrants: Latino and Asian American student victimization. *Youth & Society, 41*, 186–208.

Peguero, A. A. (2011). Immigration, schools, and violence: Assimilation and student misbehavior. *Sociological Spectrum, 31*, 695–717.

Peguero, A. A. (2012a). The children of immigrants' diminishing perceptions of just and fair punishment. *Punishment & Society, 14*, 429–451.

Peguero, A. A. (2012b). Schools, bullying, and inequality: Intersecting factors and complexities with the stratification of youth victimization at school. *Sociology Compass, 6*, 402–412.

Peguero, A. A. (2013). An adolescent victimization immigrant paradox?: School-based routines, lifestyles, and victimization across immigration generations. *Journal of Youth and Adolescence, 42*, 1759–1773.

Peguero, A. A., & Bondy, J. M. (2011). Immigration and students' relationship with teachers. *Education and Urban Society, 43*, 165–183.

Peguero, A. A., & Bondy, J. M. (2015). Schools, justice, and immigrant students: Assimilation, race, ethnicity, gender, and perceptions of fairness and order. *Teachers College Record, 117*, 1–42.

Peguero, A. A., & Hong, J. S. (2019). Are violence and disorder at school placing adolescents within immigrant families at higher risk of dropping out? *Journal of School Violence, 18*(2), 241–258.

Portes, A., & Rumbaut, R. (2014). *Immigrant America: A portrait.* Berkeley, CA: University of California Press.

Rios, V. M. (2011). *Punished: Policing the lives of Black and Latino boys.* New York: New York University Press.

Rios, V. M. (2017). *Human targets: Schools, police, and the criminalization of Latino youth.* Chicago, IL: The University of Chicago Press.

Schildkraut, J., & Muschert, G. W. (2019). *Columbine, 20 years later and beyond: Lessons from tragedy.* Santa Barbara, CA: Praeger.

Shedd, C. (2015). *Unequal city: Race, schools, and perceptions of injustice.* New York: Russell Sage Foundation.

Tanner-Smith, E. E., Fisher, B. W., Addington, L. A., & Gardella, J. H. (2018). Adding security, but subtracting safety? Exploring schools' use of multiple visible security measures. *American Journal of Criminal Justice, 43*(1), 102–119.

United States Census Bureau. (2017). *Current population survey.* Washington, DC: United States Census Bureau, Population Division.

United States Department of Education. (2015). *Educational services for immigrant children and those recently arrived to the United States.* Retrieved from https://www2.ed.gov/policy/rights/guid/unaccompanied-children.html

Chapter 2

How Immigration Matters With School Violence and Safety

We start this chapter with a brief overview of how immigration matters with regard to school violence and safety. First, we provide the definition and perspective about school violence and safety that are incorporated in this book. Second, we discuss the significance of the context of reception for immigrants and their children. Third, we highlight the complexities and details surrounding the "immigrant criminal" myth, as well as how it matters in regard to violence and safety for immigrants and their children. Fourth, we describe the growing phenomena of the school to prison/deportation pipeline. Fifth, we depict the social, political, and educational climate of immigration and its relevance to the circumstances and opportunities immigrants and their children experience. Sixth, we explain theories of assimilation, such as straight-line, segmented, and immigrant optimism hypotheses, and explain their relevance within schools.

2.1 Defining School Violence and Safety

Before we delve into discussing how immigration matters with school violence and safety, it is first important to discuss our foundation, definitions, and parameters of school violence and safety, especially as they could pertain to how the children of immigrants are considered a vulnerable and marginalized population. The National Institute of Education (NIE) *Safe School Study* (1978) report to Congress is one of the first studies to focus on assessing the level of violence occurring within U.S. schools. The landmark study, which was mandated by Congress, contained information obtained from a total of 31,373 students, 23,895 teachers, and 15,894 principals in the United States in 1976–1977. The *Safe School Study* suggests that violence occurring within schools is not prominently committed by "outsiders" but rather by the students themselves. Thus, the NIE *Safe School Study* clearly denotes that school administrators and policymakers can indeed implement policies to ameliorate violence occurring within schools and among members of the school community. Policy changes suggested to facilitate an administrator's objective of reducing violence at school include increasing efforts in student governance and rule through enforcement, treating students fairly and equally, improving the relevance of subject matter to suit students' interests and needs, and reducing class size. The study also presents results reflecting that unemployment, poverty, and neighborhood conditions are not imperative factors of the violence occurring within a school; rather, school characteristics, such as size of student enrollment, student-teacher ratios, and principals' fairness, firmness, and consistency of discipline are more relevant in reducing school violence (Gottfredson, 2001; May, 2014; Mayer & Jimerson, 2018; Muschert & Peguero, 2010; Muschert, Henry, Bracy, & Peguero, 2013; NIE, 1978).

Since the 1978 NIE *Safe School Study* report to Congress, researchers have continued to explore the possible causes, related factors, and consequences of school violence. As researchers began to scrutinize the landmark study, the relative definitions of school violence and the associated policies changed. Conventional research, such as the aforementioned 1978 NIE study, utilized a definition of school violence that is founded on legal statutes of crime, such as murder, rape, assault, robbery, and theft; however, the definition of school violence that typically applies to the adult realm is an inappropriate framework toward identifying, understanding, and addressing youth violence within schools (Gottfredson, 2001; May, 2014; Mayer & Jimerson, 2018; Muschert & Peguero, 2010; Muschert et al., 2013). Given different psychological and sociological circumstances, the effects of victimization and harm from violence that youth endure are comparatively more damaging to children's development than to adults (Cohen & Espelage, 2020; Finkelhor, 2014). Research clearly indicates that youth have limited mental capacity and are thus less able to defend and protect themselves than adults (Cohen & Espelage, 2020; Finkelhor, 2014). A seemingly less severe instance of victimization may cause a child to suffer emotional, mental, and physical injury to an extent that an adult would not (Cohen & Espelage, 2020; Finkelhor, 2014). This new perspective from developmental researchers draws into question the school's culture of tolerance for behaviors such as bullying, sexual harassment, racial and ethnic bias treatment, body image, religious persecution, and the like, not only among the student body but also from administrators, faculty, and staff (Cohen & Espelage, 2020; Gottfredson, 2001; May, 2014; Mayer & Jimerson, 2018; Muschert & Peguero, 2010; Muschert et al., 2013). Such behaviors, as well as the social and cultural practices or policies that sustain these behaviors, are consequently no longer tolerated as a normal part of the school experience for students but rather tend to be more strongly scrutinized than in the past (Cohen & Espelage, 2020; Gottfredson, 2001; May, 2014; Mayer & Jimerson, 2018; Muschert & Peguero, 2010; Muschert et al., 2013). In addition, in distinct parts of this book, the relationship between offending and victimization will be discussed simultaneously because the offending and victimization phenomenon is symbiotic, especially in association within the school context. For example, Melde and Esbensen (2009) examined a nationally representative sample of 250 schools and found that engagement in school-based misbehavior is a strong predictor of school-based victimization. In other words, victimization and offending, albeit two distinct phenomena, will be at times conflated because both are known to have a derailing influence on positive development and educational progress (Cohen & Espelage, 2020; Finkelhor, 2014; Gottfredson, 2001; Melde & Esbensen, 2009; Musu, Zhang, Wang, Zhang, & Oudekerk, 2018).

Therefore, we will incorporate an approach highlighting the broad definition of school violence that includes student-on-student violent victimization, harassment, hate-motivated speech, bullying, and the like, but also biased treatment by administrators, faculty, and staff, as potential forms of violence. As noted, it is evident that school policies and practices that do not promote fair and just treatment of all students undermine the pursuits of establishing a safe and healthy learning environment for all students (Cohen & Espelage, 2020; Gottfredson, 2001; May, 2014; Mayer & Jimerson, 2018; Muschert & Peguero, 2010; Muschert et al., 2013; Peguero, 2012b). As we will discuss in detail throughout this book, the children of immigrants face and endure experiences that are violent and marginalizing and that undermine their safety and educational pursuits while at school.

2.2 Context of Reception

As it is commonly known and often referred to, the United States is a nation of immigrants. Over the past 300 years, even before it was formed as a nation, immigrants migrated to the United States for a wide array of reasons, including war, poverty, and religious persecution (Kasinitz, Mollenkopf, Waters, & Holdaway, 2009; Louie,

2012; Portes & Rumbaut, 2014; Suárez-Orozco, Suárez-Orozco, & Todorova, 2009). It is also important that "forced" migration to the United States in the context of slavery is part of this nation's history, and the damages sustained are still occurring (Kasinitz et al., 2009; Lee & Zhou, 2015; Louie, 2012; Portes & Rumbaut, 2014; Suárez-Orozco et al., 2009). Nevertheless, the historic, persistent, and current narrative mainly emphasizes that the idea of immigrating to the United States is one of economic opportunity and fortune (Kasinitz et al., 2009; Lee & Zhou, 2015; Portes & Rumbaut, 2014; Suárez-Orozco et al., 2009). Throughout U.S. history, it is true that there have been ebbs and flows of immigrants coming to the United States seeking economic opportunity; however, for the most part, the better economic opportunities were available historically and predominantly to immigrants from Western European countries in the form of well-paying, blue-collar manufacturer employment (Kasinitz et al., 2009; Lee & Zhou, 2015; Portes & Rumbaut, 2014; Suárez-Orozco et al., 2009).

In 1965, however, a significant immigration policy shift increased the flow of immigrants from Asia, the Caribbean, South America, and Africa (Kasinitz et al., 2009; Lee & Zhou, 2015; Louie, 2012; Okamoto, 2014; Portes & Rumbaut, 2014; Telles & Ortiz, 2009). But with this immigration wave, it is argued that the context of reception has shifted because the economic opportunities and jobs that were historically available for new immigrants have changed in a post-industrial era to low-wage service jobs (Kasinitz et al., 2009; Lee & Zhou, 2015; Louie, 2012; Okamoto, 2014; Portes & Rumbaut, 2014; Telles & Ortiz, 2009). Moreover, in a post-industrial U.S. context, historically immigrant-rich areas, such as New York, California, and Florida, are no longer the primary destinations for immigrants – a huge proportion of them now residing in destination areas, such as North Carolina, Virginia, and Georgia, in the pursuit of economic and employment opportunities (Lee & Zhou, 2015; Louie, 2012; Okamoto, 2014; Portes & Rumbaut, 2014; Telles & Ortiz, 2009). This is significant because these newer immigration destination areas are social and cultural contexts that do not have a history of immigration and thus may not have the resources or understanding or be otherwise equipped to manage all the complexities associated with providing a welcoming context of reception for immigrants and their children, especially – for the purposes of this book – in schools.

As a result of migration to the United States, immigrants and their children are often considered to be more at risk for maltreatment due to the stress and pressure that they and their families experience in the migration process (Golash-Boza, 2012, 2015; Gonzales, 2016; Portes & Rumbaut, 2014; Suárez-Orozco et al., 2009). It is critical to point out that for many immigrants and their children, the immigration experience constitutes a drastic life transition that often engenders fear, loss, isolation, confusion, and uncertainty about the present and future (Golash-Boza, 2012, 2015; Gonzales, 2016; Portes & Rumbaut, 2014; Suárez-Orozco et al., 2009). As noted, although there are countless reasons for migration, such as war, famine, religious persecution, and disaster, the process of leaving one's home, country, and culture is not a single event (Golash-Boza, 2012, 2015; Gonzales, 2016; Portes & Rumbaut, 2014; Suárez-Orozco et al., 2009). Rather, educators should be reminded that migration is a lengthy and difficult process that can involve danger for children and their families (Golash-Boza, 2012, 2015; Gonzales, 2016; Portes & Rumbaut, 2014; Suárez-Orozco et al., 2009). As we will note throughout this book, many immigrants and their children are vulnerable to marginalization, exploitation, and violence during the immigration process (Golash-Boza, 2012, 2015; Gonzales, 2016; Portes & Rumbaut, 2014; Suárez-Orozco et al., 2009). Language barriers, racism, biased treatment, prejudice, xenophobia, and unfamiliar customs are all part of the social and cultural experiences for the children of immigrants (Golash-Boza, 2012, 2015; Gonzales, 2016; Portes & Rumbaut, 2014). Therefore, it is crucial to understand the distinct factors associated with school safety and violence for the children of immigrants.

2.3 "Immigrant Criminal" Myth

Because this book focuses on the significance of immigration and its association with school violence and safety, we must also discuss the potential role of the "immigrant criminal" myth. It is a global phenomenon that many of a society's problems are blamed on immigrants (Chavez, 2013; Golash-Boza, 2015; Kubrin, Zatz, & Martínez, 2012; Portes & Rumbaut, 2014; Sampson, 2008). For instance, immigrants and their families have been accused of stealing jobs from hard-working natives, as well as draining resources associated with public services (e.g., health care and education). Moreover, there is a perception that immigrants and their families bring with them disease and violence (Chavez, 2013; Golash-Boza, 2015; Kubrin et al., 2012; Portes & Rumbaut, 2014; Sampson, 2008). This belief about an immigrant and crime or violence link is historic and persistent (Chavez, 2013;

Golash-Boza, 2015; Kubrin et al., 2012; Portes & Rumbaut, 2014; Sampson, 2008). Many scholars argue that the "immigrant criminal" is a myth and stereotype that has real and detrimental effects on immigrants and their families (Chavez, 2013; Golash-Boza, 2015; Kubrin et al., 2012; Portes & Rumbaut, 2014; Sampson, 2008).

The Children of Immigrants Longitudinal Study (CILS) was designed to study the adaptation process of the immigrant second generation. The original survey was conducted with large samples of second-generation immigrant children attending the eighth and ninth grades in public and private schools in the metropolitan areas of Miami/Ft. Lauderdale in Florida and in San Diego, California. The total sample size was 5,262. Respondents came from 77 different nationalities, although the sample reflects the most sizable immigrant nationalities in each area. A number of studies analyzed this data to explore the immigration and crime link. One 2006 study utilizing CILS data, however, gained much social attention. A report titled "Debunking the Myth of Immigrant Criminality: Imprisonment Among First- and Second-Generation Young Men" by Portes and Rumbaut (2014) indicated that immigrants have the lowest rates of imprisonment for criminal convictions in American society. Both the national- and local-level findings presented here turn conventional wisdom on its head and present a challenge to criminological theory, as well as to sociological perspectives.

There are a number of research studies indicating that increases in violence and crime at the individual, community, and structural levels are not linked to immigration; to the contrary, immigration is argued to be associated with decreases in violence and crime (Kubrin et al., 2012; Martínez, 2014; Martínez & Valenzuela, 2006; Portes & Rumbaut, 2014; Sampson, 2008). At the individual level, immigrants are less likely to engage in delinquent and criminal activity, as well as drink and/or use illicit substances (Kubrin et al., 2012; Martínez, 2014; Martínez & Valenzuela, 2006; Portes & Rumbaut, 2014; Sampson, 2008). Research also demonstrates that as the immigrant population increases within a community, violent and property crime rates decrease (Kubrin et al., 2012; Martínez, 2014; Martínez & Valenzuela, 2006; Portes & Rumbaut, 2014; Sampson, 2008). At the structural level, Ewing, Martínez, and Rumbaut (2015) report that

> roughly 1.6 percent of immigrant males 18–39 are incarcerated, compared to 3.3 percent of the native-born. The disparity in incarceration rates has existed for decades, as evidenced by data

from the 1980, 1990, and 2000 decennial Census . . . incarceration rates of the native-born were anywhere from two to five times higher than that of immigrants.

(p. 1)

Although there is much evidence "debunking" the immigrant criminal myth, this does not mean that the myth has ceased to have detrimental effects on immigrants and their children.

Although the immigrant criminal myth suggests a direct link between being an immigrant and criminality, immigrants are more often the targets of harassment, hate crimes, and crime in general (Chavez, 2013; Golash-Boza, 2015; Gonzales, 2016; Kubrin et al., 2012). Moreover, immigrants and their families are fearful of admitting that they have been a victim of a crime in part because of fear of deportation from the United States if they report the crime (Chavez, 2013; Golash-Boza, 2015; Gonzales, 2016; Menjívar & Bejarano, 2004). As a result, criminal offenders take advantage of immigrants' reluctance to report crime as a vulnerability to interpersonal violence, robbery, and sexual assaults (Kubrin et al., 2012; Martínez, 2014; Menjívar & Bejarano, 2004). Some native-born individuals and groups view immigrants as a threat to their jobs and resources, which results in hate-based interpersonal violence (Chavez, 2013; Martínez, 2014). To this end, the general social discourse of anti-immigrant sentiments and the immigrant criminal myth are finding their way into schools and impacting the children of immigrants' educational experiences.

2.4 School to Prison/Deportation Pipeline

The school to prison pipeline is an important and debated topic in the U.S. school system (King, Rujosa, & Peguero, 2018; Marchbanks, Peguero, Varela, Blake, & Eason, 2018; Rios, 2011, 2017; Varela, Peguero, Eason, Marchbanks, & Blake, 2018). In recent history, U.S. researchers from across multiple fields have investigated if there is a relationship between punishment school policies and the growing mass incarceration. Some argue that the increase in punitive school policies pushes students out of schools and does so in a manner that raises their likelihood of long-term contact with the U.S. juvenile and/or adult justice system (King et al., 2018; Marchbanks et al., 2018; Rios, 2011, 2017; Varela et al., 2018). Research findings indicate that the school to prison pipeline disproportionately affects students of color, who are

punished in schools at higher rates than their White American counterparts (Marchbanks et al., 2018; Rios, 2011, 2017; Shedd, 2015;
Varela et al., 2018). As a testament to the salience of this phenomenon,
in 2014, the U.S. Departments of Justice and Education established
a national initiative to ameliorate and address the school to prison
pipeline, especially the disproportionate impact on racial and ethnic
minority students (King et al., 2018).

There is emerging evidence that the children of immigrants are also
experiencing disproportionate rates of school discipline and punishment. Peguero and colleagues (2015) report that once other student
and school characteristics are controlled for in the model, the children of immigrants are not misbehaving more at school than their
White American counterparts; however, the children of immigrants
have increased odds of being punished at school. Moreover, Peguero
and Hong (2019) indicate that the effect of that school punishment is
relatively more detrimental for the children of immigrants.

Apparently, the children of immigrants are more likely to attend
schools with increased levels of security, law enforcement presence, and
strictness (Gonzales, 2016; Peguero, 2011; Peguero et al., 2020; Verma,
Maloney, & Austin, 2017). Moreover, in a recent study, Peguero and
colleagues (2020) have revealed that the children of immigrants have a
relatively increased exposure to having contact with the juvenile and
criminal justice systems while at school. In turn, it is plausible that the
disproportionate contact that the children of immigrants have with the
criminal and juvenile justice systems could facilitate the deportation
of undocumented children of immigrants. There is emerging research
that suggests a school to deportation pipeline. In one study, Verma
and colleagues (2017) indicate that a significant number of children
of immigrants find themselves in deportation hearings, which include
families seeking political asylum or amnesty from undocumented status. Studies have suggested that schoolteachers, administrators, and staff
have taken on the role of surveilling and reporting immigrant students
who are suspected to be undocumented to the immigration authorities (Gonzales, 2011, 2016; Gonzales, Suárez-Orozco, & Dedios-
Sanguineti, 2013; Verma et al., 2017). In the next chapter, there will
be a deeper discussion about the complexities with the marginalization
and vulnerabilities associated with being undocumented in regards to
youth safety and well-being at school; however, it is becoming quite
evident that the emergence of a school to prison/deportation pipeline
is indeed a real problem for the children of immigrants.

2.5 Social, Political, and Educational Climate of Immigration

The debate over immigration is a complex issue that is often discussed with biased views and conflicting information. Much of this debate is centered on an immigration crime, employment, and educational link (Gonzales, 2016; Kubrin et al., 2012; Portes & Rumbaut, 2014; Suárez-Orozco et al., 2009). As noted in the prior section, even though there is a ubiquitous stereotype of immigrants as deviant, criminal, and unintelligent, research reveals evidence to the contrary. The children of immigrants are less likely to be involved in crime, substance use, and general deviance (Kubrin et al., 2012; Martínez & Valenzuela, 2006; Portes & Rumbaut, 2014; Sampson, 2008). Immigrant youth are also educationally outperforming their U.S. native-born counterparts (Kao, Vaquera, & Goyette, 2013; Portes & Rumbaut, 2014; Rong & Preissle, 2008; Suárez-Orozco et al., 2009). In fact, the children of immigrants have increased beliefs that hard work, progress, and success within school will lead to adult educational and economic success (Kao et al., 2013; Louie, 2012; Portes & Rumbaut, 2014; Suárez-Orozco et al., 2009). Unfortunately, however, it appears that the discourse that vilifies immigrants and their children could be seeping into schools.

The children of immigrants are often subjected to negative treatment, such as biased treatment, ridicule, and harassment from other students, as well as teachers and school administrators (Gutierrez, 2014; Lee, 2005, 2009; Olsen, 2008; Peguero, 2009; Portes & Rumbaut, 2014). The children of immigrants are often placed in classes or academic tracks far below the mainstream classes, which in turn hinders their educational advancement and success (Gutierrez, 2014; Olsen, 2008; Suárez-Orozco et al., 2009, Suárez-Orozco, Darbes, Dias, & Sutin, 2011). Outside perceptions of low academic ability, along with rejection by peers and fear for personal safety, are all reflective of the children of immigrants' experiences within the U.S. school system (Hong et al., 2015; Lee, 2005, 2009; Olsen, 2008; Peguero, 2009; Suárez-Orozco et al., 2009, 2011). Moreover, it appears that teachers within classrooms can sometimes present barriers against the children of immigrants' pursuit of educational success.

Some teachers view the children of immigrants as problems within their classrooms, burdened by their supposed lacking capabilities, and argue that the children of immigrants diminish the teacher's ability to educate all students effectively and efficiently. Teachers often hold negative and unwelcoming attitudes toward the children of immigrants being placed in their classes (Goodwin, 2017; Olsen, 2008; Peguero & Bondy, 2011; Pettit, 2011; Suárez-Orozco et al., 2009). A few rationalizations for holding negative or unwelcoming views include the chronic lack of time to address the unique needs of the children of immigrants, perceived intensification of teacher workloads when the children of immigrants are enrolled in their classes, and feelings of professional inadequacy to work with immigrant children (Goodwin, 2017; Kao et al., 2013; Louie, 2012; Olsen, 2008; Pettit, 2011). Because of the perception that the children of immigrants restrict the advancement and educational progress for the entire class is not uncommon within U.S. schools, teachers can be reluctant to accept, have, keep, and teach the children of immigrants in their classrooms.

We would be remiss to not also discuss the impact of the 45th presidential administration on the social, political, and educational climate of immigration. Since Donald Trump took office in 2016, he has promised to deport 11 million undocumented immigrants, build a wall between Mexico and the United States, end birthright citizenship, and withhold federal funds from sanctuary cities or cities that have decided to limit their cooperation with the national government's attempts to enforce immigration law in order to protect low-priority immigrants from deportation. The Trump administration has also semantically linked undocumented, Latina/o, and African immigrants with criminality, feces, and diseases (Beckwith, 2018; Walker, 2015). While schools have never been immune to immigration politics, they have been increasingly negatively impacted by the broader forces of xenophobia under the Trump administration. For example, during Trump's presidential campaign, his hostile political rhetoric has an adverse impact on the children of immigrants, such as creating startling levels of fear and increasing racial and ethnic tensions in classrooms (Costello, 2016a). Since his election, educators across the United States have reported changes in school climates that include hostile remarks, such as "Go back to [insert foreign country name here, usually Mexico]" (Vara-Orta, 2018, para. 13), "Trump is going to throw you back over the wall, you know?" (Costello, 2016b, p. 6), and "Put the panic back in Hispanic" (Sharp, 2017) made to immigrant youth, particularly those who are Latina/o. Teachers have also reported that students' concerns for their own or family members' deportation have increased exponentially (Ee & Gándara, 2020; Rogers et al., 2017; Sanchez, Freeman, & Martin, 2018) and that some students carry their birth certificates and Social Security cards to school (Costello, 2016b). Schools play an important role in defining the necessary qualities of inclusion and belonging in the United States, particularly for the children of immigrants (Goodwin, 2017; Rong & Preissle, 2008). As racial and ethnic hostility intensifies in schools, researchers and practitioners committed to school safety for the children of immigrants must address the socio-political context of their schooling experiences.

2.6 Theories of Assimilation

U.S. schools are one of the fundamental social institutions with which immigrants and their children first come into contact. Without a doubt, U.S. schools have undergone phenomenal transformations, with changes in educational philosophy, instruction, and curriculum as a result of the many historical immigration waves to this nation (Kao et al., 2013; Olsen, 2008; Rong & Preissle, 2008; Suárez-Orozco et al., 2009); however, the scholastic approach, as well as the ideological role of the school, toward educating and socializing students in immigrant families has been historically debated. At the center of this debate between schools and immigration are continuing fundamental questions about who is "American," how to become one, at what pace, and how the school facilitates the process of assimilation (Kao et al., 2013; Olsen, 2008; Rong & Preissle, 2008; Suárez-Orozco et al., 2009). For the purposes of this book, as well as guided by prior research, we will define generational status as the following: generational status indicates whether the youth/student is first, second, or third-plus generation. First-generation youth are born outside the United States, second-generation youth are born in the United States and have at least one parent born outside the United States, and third-plus-generation or native-born youth are born, as are both of their parents, in the United States. Subsequently, assimilation has been the historical educational model toward socializing students in immigrant families in U.S. society. Three theoretical frameworks have emerged from this debate about assimilation and schooling that will be at the center of this research analysis: straight-line assimilation, segmented assimilation, and the immigrant optimism hypothesis.

Straight-Line Assimilation. Conventional or straight-line assimilation theorists argue that the assimilation process involves immigrants assimilating to the dominant host culture, and in turn, the assimilation process facilitates upward mobility for immigrants (Alba & Foner,

2015; Alba & Nee, 2003; Glazer & Moynihan, 1970; Kasinitz et al., 2009). Under this straight-line assimilation process, it is given that immigrants who assimilate to the dominant host culture will achieve employment, residential, and educational success. This straight-line assimilation perspective suggests that across generations, the children of immigrants from diverse backgrounds come to share a common culture and become indistinguishable from their native-born peers. The children of immigrants are expected to resign their distinct cultural values and beliefs and relocate out of ethnic enclaves in order to earn improved economic and educational opportunities that will result in higher achievement and attainment across immigrant generations (Alba & Foner, 2015; Alba & Nee, 2003; Glazer & Moynihan, 1970; Kasinitz et al., 2009).

Segmented Assimilation. Segmented assimilationists contend that the process of straight-line assimilation no longer depicts the opportunities for and access to social mobility immigrants and their children currently have in the United States. Segmented assimilation theorists describe a process of assimilation that results in various social, economic, and educational outcomes, which may reflect a path of upward or downward mobility (Lee, 2005, 2009; Lee & Zhou, 2015; Portes & Rumbaut, 2014; Suárez-Orozco et al., 2009; Waters, 2001). Segmented assimilationists propose that the assimilation process is segmented into several divergent forms of adaptation: assimilation into the White middle class; preservation of ethnic cultural traditions and close ethnic ties through social networks in the community, also referred to as ethnic enclaves; and assimilation into the underclass, also referred to as a second-generation decline. Within a segmented assimilation conceptual framework, assimilating and incorporating the dominant group's values and beliefs may place immigrants on distinct trajectories, one of which may be on a path of marginalization, poverty, and failure (Lee, 2005, 2009; Lee & Zhou, 2015; Portes & Rumbaut, 2014; Suárez-Orozco et al., 2009; Waters, 2001).

Immigrant Optimism. The final conceptual framework to be presented in this study is the "immigrant optimism" hypothesis. Kao and Tienda (1995) emphasize the progress of immigrant origin groups over successive generations. But unlike straight-line assimilation or segmented assimilation approaches, this framework stresses the relative overachievements of the second generation compared with the first and third-plus generations, particularly the third-plus majority population. This approach differs by denoting that educational achievement is associated with achievement or optimism of immigrant parents who communicate and emphasize high educational aspirations and expectations to their children (Feliciano, 2006; Kao & Tienda, 1995; Peguero & Bondy, 2015). In other words, immigrants often bring with them a culture of optimism because the motivation for migrating to the United States is one of hope and opportunity. Immigrant parents relay an optimistic belief to their children by highlighting that life in the United States is significantly better than life in their native country of origin. This model implies that the second generation will have higher educational and occupational attainments than either the first generation or third-plus generations.

In this chapter, we provided the definition of and perspectives about school violence and safety that are incorporated in our book. We discussed the importance of the context of reception for immigrants and their children and the implications for their school safety. We highlighted the complexities and details surrounding the "immigrant criminal" myth, as well as how it matters in regard to violence and safety for immigrants and their children, and implications for a "school to prison/deportation pipeline." We presented how social, political, and educational climate concerning immigration can impact school safety for the children of immigrants but also for all students. We explained theories of assimilation, such as straight-line, segmented, and immigrant optimism, to guide readers toward understanding the connections between immigration and school safety.

References

Alba, R., & Foner, N. (2015). *Strangers no more: Immigration and the challenges of integration in North America and Western Europe*. Princeton, NJ: Princeton University Press.

Alba, R., & Nee, V. (2003). *Remaking the American mainstream: Assimilation and contemporary immigration*. Boston, MA: Harvard University Press.

Beckwith, R. T. (2018, January 11). President Trump called El Salvador, Haiti "shithole" countries: Report. *Time*. Retrieved from http://time.com/5100058/donald-trump-shithole-countries/

Chavez, L. (2013). *The Latino threat: Constructing immigrants, citizens and the nation*. Stanford, CA: Stanford University Press.

Cohen, J., & Espelage, D. L. (2020). *Feeling safe in school: Bullying and violence prevention around the world*. Cambridge, MA: Harvard Education Press.

Costello, M. B. (2016a). *The Trump effect: The impact of the presidential campaign on our nation's schools*. Montgomery, AL: Southern Poverty Law Center.

Costello, M. B. (2016b). *After election day the Trump effect: The impact of the 2016 election on our nation's schools*. Montgomery, AL: Southern Poverty Law Center.

Ee, J., & Gándara, P. (2020). The impact of immigration enforcement on the nation's schools. *American Educational Research Journal, 57*(2). Advance online publication.

Ewing, W. A., Martínez, D. E., & Rumbaut, R. (2015). *The criminalization of immigration in the United States*. Washington, DC: American Immigration Council.

Feliciano, C. (2006). *Unequal origins: Immigrant selection and the education of the second generation*. New York: LFB Scholarly Publishing.

Finkelhor, D. (2014). *Childhood victimization: Violence, crime and abuse in the lives of young people*. New York: Oxford University Press.

Glazer, N., & Moynihan, D. P. (1970). *Beyond the melting pot*. Cambridge, MA: MIT Press.

Golash-Boza, T. (2012). *Immigration nation: Raids, detentions, and deportations in post–9/11 America*. Boulder, CO: Paradigm.

Golash-Boza, T. (2015). *Deported: Immigrant policing, disposable labor, and global capitalism*. New York: New York University Press.

Gonzales, R. G. (2011). Learning to be illegal: Undocumented youth and shifting legal contexts in the transition to adulthood. *American Sociological Review, 76*, 602–619.

Gonzales, R. G. (2016). *Lives in limbo: Undocumented and coming of age in America*. Berkeley, CA: University of California Press.

Gonzales, R. G., Suárez-Orozco, C., & Dedios-Sanguineti, M. C. (2013). Contextualizing concepts of mental health among undocumented immigrant youth in the United States. *American Behavioral Scientist, 57*, 1173–1198.

Goodwin, A. L. (2017). Who's in the classroom now? Teacher preparation and the education of immigrant children. *Educational Studies, 53*(5), 433–449.

Gottfredson, D. C. (2001). *Schools and delinquency*. New York: Cambridge University Press.

Gutierrez, L. A. (2014). Youth social justice engagement in the face of anti-Latina/o immigrant illegitimacy. *Urban Review, 47*, 307–323.

Hong, J. S., Merrin, G. J., Crosby, S., Jozefowicz, D. M., Lee, J. M., & Allen-Meares, P. (2015). Individual and contextual factors associated with immigrant youth feeling unsafe in school: A social-ecological analysis. *Journal of Immigrant and Minority Health*, 1–11.

Kao, G., & Tienda, M. (1995). Optimism and achievement: The educational performance of immigrant youth. *Social Science Quarterly, 76*, 1–19.

Kao, G., Vaquera, E., & Goyette, K. (2013). *Education and immigration*. Malden, MA: Policy Press.

Kasinitz, P., Mollenkopf, J. H., Waters, M. C., & Holdaway, J. (2009). *Inheriting the city: The children of immigrants come of age*. New York: Russell Sage Foundation.

King, S., Rujosa, A., & Peguero, A. A. (2018). The school-to-prison pipeline. In J. Deakin, E. Taylor, & A. Kupchik (Eds.), *The Palgrave international handbook of school discipline, surveillance and social control*. London: Palgrave Macmillan.

Kubrin, C., Zatz, M., & Martínez, R. (2012). *Punishing immigrants: Policy, politics, and injustice*. New York: New York University Press.

Lee, S. J. (2005). *Up against Whiteness: Race, school and immigrant youth*. New York: Teachers College Press.

Lee, S. J. (2009). *Unraveling the model minority stereotype: Listening to Asian American youth*. New York: Teachers College Press.

Lee, S. J., & Zhou, M. (2015). *The Asian American achievement paradox*. New York: Russell Sage Foundation.

Louie, V. (2012). *Keeping the immigrant bargain: The costs and rewards of success in America*. New York: Russell Sage Foundation.

Marchbanks, M. P., Peguero, A. A., Varela, K. S., Blake, J. J., & Eason, J. M. (2018). School strictness and disproportionate minority contact: Investigating racial and ethnic disparities with the "school-to-prison pipeline." *Youth Violence and Juvenile Justice, 16*(2), 241–259.

Martínez, R. (2014). *Latino homicide: Immigration, violence and community*. New York: Routledge Falmer.

Martínez, R., & Valenzuela, A. (2006). *Immigration and crime: Race, ethnicity and violence*. New York: New York University Press.

May, D. C. (2014). *School safety in America: A reasoned look at the rhetoric*. Durham: Carolina Academic Press.

Mayer, M. J., & Jimerson, S. R. (2018). *School safety and violence prevention: Science, practice and policy*. Washington, DC: American Psychological Association.

Melde, C., & Esbensen, F. A. (2009). The victim – offender overlap and fear of in-school victimization: A longitudinal examination of risk assessment models. *Crime & Delinquency, 55*, 499–525.

Menjívar, C., & Bejarano, C. (2004). Latino immigrants' perceptions of crime and police authorities in the United States: A case study from the Phoenix metropolitan area. *Ethnic and Racial Studies, 27*(1), 120–148.

Muschert, G. W., Henry, S., Bracy, N. L., & Peguero, A. A. (2013). *Responses to school violence: Confronting the Columbine effect*. Boulder, CO: Lynne Reinner Publishers.

Muschert, G. W., & Peguero, A. A. (2010). The Columbine effect and school anti-violence policy. *Research in Social Problems & Public Policy, 17*, 117–148.

Musu, L., Zhang, A., Wang, K., Zhang, J., & Oudekerk, B. A. (2019). *Indicators of school crime and safety: 2018*. NCES 2019-047/NCJ 252571. Washington, DC: National Center for Education Statistics, U.S. Department of Education, and Bureau of Justice Statistics, Office of Justice Programs, U.S. Department of Justice.

National Institute of Education. (1978). *Violent schools, safe schools: The safe school study report to congress*. Washington, DC: U.S. Government Printing Office.

Okamoto, D. G. (2014). *Redefining race: Asian American panethnicity and shifting ethnic boundaries*. New York: Russell Sage Foundation.

Olsen, L. (2008). *Made in America: Immigrant students in our public schools*. New York: New York University Press.

Peguero, A. A. (2009). Victimizing the children of immigrants: Latino and Asian American student victimization. *Youth & Society, 41*, 186–208.

Peguero, A. A. (2011). Immigration, schools, and violence: Assimilation and student misbehavior. *Sociological Spectrum, 31*, 695–717.

Peguero, A. A. (2012b). Schools, bullying, and inequality: Intersecting factors and complexities with the stratification of youth victimization at school. *Sociology Compass, 6,* 402–412.

Peguero, A. A., & Bondy, J. M. (2011). Immigration and students' relationship with teachers. *Education and Urban Society, 43,* 165–183.

Peguero, A. A., & Bondy, J. M. (2015). Schools, justice, and immigrant students: Assimilation, race, ethnicity, gender, and perceptions of fairness and order. *Teachers College Record, 117,* 1–42.

Peguero, A. A., Eason, J. M., Iwama, J., Zhang, J., Marchbanks, M. T., & Blake, J. J. (2020). *Immigration and school threat?: Exploring the significance of the border.* Research under review.

Peguero, A. A., & Hong, J. S. (2019). Are violence and disorder at school placing adolescents within immigrant families at higher risk of dropping out? *Journal of School Violence, 18*(2), 241–258.

Pettit, S. K. (2011). Teachers' beliefs about English language learners in the mainstream classroom: A review of the literature. *International Multilingual Research Journal, 5*(2), 123–147.

Portes, A., & Rumbaut, R. (2014). *Immigrant America: A portrait.* Berkeley, CA: University of California Press.

Rios, V. M. (2011). *Punished: Policing the lives of Black and Latino boys.* New York: New York University Press.

Rios, V. M. (2017). *Human targets: Schools, police, and the criminalization of Latino youth.* Chicago, IL: The University of Chicago Press.

Rogers, J., Franke, M., Yun, J. E., Ishimoto, M., Diera, C., Geller, R., . . . Brenes, T. (2017). *Teaching and learning in the age of Trump: Increasing stress and hostility in America's high schools.* Los Angeles, CA: UCLA's Institute for Democracy, Education, and Access.

Rong, X., & Preissle, J. (2008). *Educating immigrant students in the 21st century: What we need to know to meet the challenges.* Thousand Oaks, CA: Corwin Press.

Sampson, R. J. (2008). Rethinking crime and immigration. *Contexts, 7,* 28–33.

Sanchez, S., Freeman, R., & Martin, P. (2018). Stressed, overworked, and not sure whom to trust: How public school educators are navigating recent immigration enforcement. *The Civil Rights Project.* Retrieved from www.civilrights project.ucla.edu/research/k-12-education/immigration-immigrant-students/ stressed-overworked-and-not-sure-whom-to-trust-the-impacts-of-recent-immigration-enforcement-on-our-public-school-educators/teachers-Immig-Enforcement-DRAFT-7.pdf

Sharp, J. (2017, September 16). *"Put the panic back in Hispanic": Photo at Roberts-dale pep rally sparks criticism.* Retrieved from www.al.com/news/mobile/index. ssf/2017/09/baldwin_school_officials.html

Shedd, C. (2015). *Unequal city: Race, schools, and perceptions of injustice.* New York: Russell Sage Foundation.

Suárez-Orozco, C., Suárez-Orozco, M. M., & Todorova, I. (2009). *Learning a new land: Immigrant students in American society.* Cambridge, MA: Harvard University Press.

Suárez-Orozco, M. M., Darbes, T., Dias, S. I., & Sutin, M. (2011). Migrations and schooling. *Annual Review of Anthropology, 40*, 311–328.

Telles, E., & Ortiz, V. (2009). *Generations of exclusion: Mexican Americans, assimilation, and race.* New York: Russel Sage Foundation.

Vara-Orta, F. (2018, August 6). *Hate in schools: An in-depth look.* Retrieved from www.edweek.org/ew/projects/hate-in-schools.html

Varela, K. S., Peguero, A. A., Eason, J. M., Marchbanks, M. P., & Blake, J. J. (2018). School strictness and education: Investigating racial and ethnic educational inequalities associated with being pushed out. *Sociology of Race and Ethnicity, 4*(2), 261–280.

Verma, S., Maloney, P., & Austin, D. W. (2017). The school to deportation pipeline: The perspectives of immigrant students and their teachers on profiling and surveillance within the school system. *The Annals of the American Academy of Political and Social Science, 673*(1), 209–229.

Walker, H. (2015, July 6). Donald Trump just released epic statement raging against Mexican immigrants and "disease." *Business Insider.* Retrieved from www.businessinsider.com/donald-trumps-epic-statement-on-mexico-2015-7

Waters, M. (2001). *Black identities: West Indian immigrant dreams and American realities.* Boston, MA: Harvard University Press.

Chapter 3

Intersecting Factors Associated With Immigration and School Safety

In this chapter, we present the intersecting factors associated with immigration and school safety. As we demonstrate, the exposure to violence and victimization at school are disparate across distinct segments of the student population, especially for the children of immigrants. However, it is also evident that the population of children of immigrants attending U.S. schools is diverse. There are inequalities and disparities associated with the population of children of immigrants in terms of their school safety. We review the relevance of factors such as race, ethnicity, region of origin, gender, English language proficiency, family, and documentation status in association with school violence and safety.

Before we start with this chapter, however, it is important to discuss the intersectionality of these various factors associated with immigration and safety. Intersectionality is a conceptual approach to studying the relationships across multiple dimensions and modalities of social relationships and subject formations such as socioeconomic status, gender, race, and ethnicity (Crenshaw, 1990; Morris, 2016; Potter, 2015). A number of researchers have argued that violence is fundamentally associated with socioeconomic status, gender, race, and ethnicity, which indicates that intersectionality warrants further critical analysis (Crenshaw, 1990; Morris, 2016; Potter, 2015). For example, the concept of the intersectionality of socioeconomic status, gender, race, and ethnicity is particularly pertinent to the growing body of research on school safety (Peguero & Popp, 2012; Morris, 2016; Peguero, 2012). Thus, because previous research studies indicate that intersectionality with regard to social inequalities and disparities is important for understanding the occurrence of school violence, as well as ensuring school safety, we encourage the reader to not simply understand these presented intersecting factors as mutually exclusive but rather to be critical by utilizing how these distinct inequalities intersect with each other when considering factors associated with immigration and school safety.

3.1 Socioeconomic Status and Social Class

It is well established that there is a strong association between socioeconomic status and where individuals reside, especially in regards to disadvantaged and under-resourced communities and violence (Morenoff, Sampson, & Raudenbush, 2001; Sampson & Sharkey, 2008). Research demonstrates that youth violence, including school safety, across multiple domains and levels is associated with socioeconomic status and community violence (Brunson & Miller, 2009; Gottfredson, 2001; Peguero, 2012). Indeed, youth, especially racial and ethnic minorities, living in disadvantaged and under-resourced communities are exposed to increased levels of violence, crime, and victimization (Gottfredson, 2001; Brunson & Miller, 2009; Rojas-Gaona, Hong, & Peguero, 2016). As a consequence, at an individual student level, research demonstrates that youth are entering schools with increased trauma, which can be associated with increased engagement and vulnerability to violence and victimization at school (Brunson & Miller, 2009; Peguero, 2009; Rojas-Gaona et al., 2016). Because schools often reflect the characteristics of the community in which the school is embedded, schools situated in disadvantaged and under-resourced communities often have increased levels of violence and victimization (Brunson & Miller, 2009; Gottfredson, 2001; Rojas-Gaona et al., 2016). Socioeconomically disadvantaged and under-resourced schools also have limited capacities to provide safe and healthy learning environments (Hong, 2009; Peguero, 2012).

Studies have documented that immigrant families and their children are more likely to reside in disadvantaged and under-resourced communities (Kao, Vaquera, & Goyette, 2013; Portes & Rumbaut, 2014; Suárez-Orozco, Suárez-Orozco, & Todorova, 2009). Moreover, the children of immigrants have increased reports of experiencing economic hardships and poverty (Portes & Rumbaut, 2014; Suárez-Orozco et al., 2009). Being socioeconomically disadvantaged can place the children of immigrants in vulnerable positions within their communities and schools, increasing their exposure to violence and likelihood of victimization (Hong et al., 2014; Hong, Merrin, Peguero, Gonzalez-Prendes, & Lee, 2016; Peguero, 2009, 2011; Portes & Rumbaut, 2014). Stress due to poverty and low socioeconomic circumstances is negatively correlated with school safety outcomes among the children of immigrants and can manifest in those children being victimized, getting into fights, and being disciplined (Hong et al., 2014, 2016; Peguero & Shekarkhar, 2011).

At the school level, because the children of immigrants often reside in disadvantaged and under-resourced communities, the children of immigrants also have increased odds of attending schools with increased levels of disorder and violence (Kao et al., 2013; Peguero, 2009, 2011; Portes & Rumbaut, 2014). Additionally, researchers have stressed that education and community inequalities impose serious barriers and challenges to implement anti-violence programs within schools (Hong, 2009; Peguero, 2012). Situational contexts of violence and bullying in the community overlap and are symbiotic with schools (Brunson & Miller, 2009; Peguero, 2009; Rojas-Gaona et al., 2016). Insufficient resources necessary for training school staff or allotting time to have anti-violence training and lessons included in the curriculum, as well as the high faculty and staff turnover that typically occurs within poorer schools, all limit the possibility of implementing anti-bullying policies and practices effectively (Hong, 2009; Peguero, 2012). Therefore, the ways that socioeconomic status are associated with immigration and school safety are multifaceted and complex.

3.2 Race, Ethnicity, and Region of Origin

Unlike the immigrants who arrived in the United States at the turn of the twentieth century, immigrants today are mainly non-European. Approximately 85 percent of immigrants in the United States migrate from Latin America, Asia, Africa, the Middle East, or the Caribbean (Louie, 2012; Portes & Rumbaut, 2014; Rong & Preissle, 2008; U.S. Census Bureau, 2017; Waters, 2001). It is estimated that within 20 years, racial and ethnic minority youth will comprise more than half of the total student population in U.S. schools (U.S. Census Bureau, 2017). In the midst of this demographic shift, it is important to point out that immigrant youth enter an educational system with a persistent history of racial and ethnic inequality. As Apple and Franklin (2004) write on the history of curriculum and its relationship to social control in the United States,

> When the public school system became increasingly solidified, schools were seen as institutions that could preserve the cultural hegemony of an embattled "native" population. Education was

the way in which the community life, values, norms, and economic advantages of the powerful were to be protected. Schools could be the great engines of moral crusade to make the children of the immigrants and Blacks like "us."

(p. 63)

Researchers have historically and consistently reported the racial and ethnic inequalities embedded in many U.S. educational school processes. Racial and ethnic minority students perceive that they are unfavorably viewed in their educational capabilities or potential (Kao et al., 2013; Kumi-Yeboah, Brobbey, & Smith, 2020; Lewis & Diamond, 2015; Noguera, 2009; Waters, 2001). Racial and ethnic minority students report experiencing low teacher expectations, less access to educational resources, placement in lower educational tracks, and guidance toward low-paying employment (Kao et al., 2013; Kumi-Yeboah et al., 2020; Lewis & Diamond, 2015; Noguera, 2009; Waters, 2001). The race and ethnicity of the majority of contemporary immigrants clearly set them apart from the conventional historical trend of White European immigrants. For the current wave of immigrants, many of them have never experienced prejudice associated with their particular skin color, racial and ethnic category, or country of origin (Kumi-Yeboah et al., 2020; Portes & Rumbaut, 2014; Waters, 2001). Moreover, the diversity among the immigrant youth population also emerges in the distinctly unique challenges and barriers they face in their daily school experiences.

Generally speaking, the children of Black immigrants come from two major regions: the Caribbean islands and the African continent. The children of Caribbean Black immigrants in the United States mainly migrate from three Caribbean countries: Jamaica, Haiti, and Trinidad. The children of African immigrants in the United States primarily migrate from three countries: Nigeria, Ethiopia, and Somalia. The children of Black immigrants are clearly diverse in terms of country of origin, languages spoken, and religion. Despite the diversity among Black immigrant youth, they are often placed into one racial and ethnic category, which dismisses, invalidates, and erases their different cultural, national, linguistic, and religious heritages (Kao et al., 2013; Koch, 2007; Kumi-Yeboah et al., 2020; Portes & Rumbaut, 2014; Rong & Preissle, 2008; Waters, 2001). Further, the children of Black immigrants are confronted with racial and ethnic segregation and biased treatment within their schools and communities. Because of the U.S. history of slavery, racial segregation, and marginalization, the children of Black immigrants often attempt to distance themselves from U.S.-born African Americans. These ethnic distinctions, though, do not protect Black immigrant youth from experiencing biased practices that occur within schools (Kao et al., 2013; Koch, 2007; Kumi-Yeboah et al., 2020; Portes & Rumbaut, 2014; Rong & Preissle, 2008; Waters, 2001). There are often many social tensions between the children of Black immigrants and U.S. native-born African American youth (Koch, 2007; Kumi-Yeboah et al., 2020; Waters, 2001). As a result, the children of Black immigrants are isolated, marginalized, and disenfranchised from other racial and ethnic minority groups. Moreover, the children of Black immigrant students are at risk of being victimized and harassed at school, as well as attending schools with increased disorder (Kumi-Yeboah et al., 2020; Peguero, 2011, 2013; Waters, 2001).

Although the children of Latina/o immigrants represent one of the fastest-growing populations in the United States, the children of Latina/o immigrants are at risk for health and educational marginalization. The children of Latina/o immigrants continue to be overrepresented among those at risk for poor behavioral, physical, and mental well-being (Gonzales, 2016; Portes & Rumbaut, 2014; Suárez-Orozco et al., 2009). Within the child welfare system, the number of children of Latina/o immigrants has steadily risen over the past several years (Dettlaff, Earner, & Phillips, 2009). In U.S. schools, the children of Latina/o immigrants have the lowest rates of college enrollment; the highest rates of high school and college attrition; lower achievement scores, educational attainment, and educational aspirations; and are three times more likely to drop out in comparison to White students (Gonzales, 2016; Portes & Rumbaut, 2014; Suárez-Orozco et al., 2009). Moreover, the children of Latina/o immigrant students are at risk of being victimized and harassed at school, as well as attending schools with increased disorder (Hong et al., 2014; Peguero, 2009, 2011, 2013; Peguero & Jiang, 2014).

The stereotype of the "model immigrant" is often assigned to the children of Asian immigrants; however, that label is detrimental. Although the children of Asian immigrants are stereotypically portrayed as academic and economic overachievers, Asian immigrant families often live in poverty, underserved by human services, underpaid, and, often, subjected to biased treatment and harassment (Kao et al., 2013; Lee, 2005, 2009; Lee & Zhou, 2015). Moreover, due to teacher expectations and the "model minority syndrome," teachers often assume that the children of Asian immigrants do not need help or assistance because of their stereotyped "natural" or "biological" ability (Kao et al., 2013; Lee, 2005, 2009; Lee & Zhou, 2015). Additionally, the children of Asian immigrants indicate that they are being "pushed" into particular academic subjects, such as math and science, in order to be accepted by school administrators, faculty, and staff; otherwise, the children of Asian immigrants are harassed, "put down," and inequitably treated (Kao et al., 2013; Lee, 2005, 2009; Lee & Zhou, 2015). As a result, the children of Asian immigrants often do not get the assistance, mentoring, guidance, and support often needed in pursuit of educational achievement and attainment. Moreover, the children of Asian immigrant students are at risk of being victimized and harassed at school, as well as attending schools with increased disorder (Hong et al., 2014; Koo et al., 2012; Peguero, 2009, 2011, 2012, 2013; Peguero & Jiang, 2014).

The children of Arab immigrants have migrated to the United States primarily because of wars, such as the Gulf War, Iraq-Iran War, and the U.S. invasions of Iraq and Afghanistan. Although ongoing political events have drawn attention to the Arab world, greater media coverage and news reports have not translated into increased research and improved understanding of Arab culture, particularly within the United States and its school system (Abu El-Haj, 2006; Golash-Boza, 2012; Haboush, 2007; Rong & Preissle, 2008). In other words, there is little research and consideration extended to the educational experiences of the children of Arab immigrants. Although research indicates that Arab immigrant families tend to be well educated relative to the American population as a whole, reflecting a high value placed on education (Abu El-Haj, 2006; Haboush, 2007; Rong & Preissle, 2008), the school experiences of the children of Arab immigrants are frequently characterized by marginalization. Without a doubt, the events of September 11, 2001, have significantly exacerbated an already well-established negative stereotype of Arab culture. As a result, the victimization, harassment, and verbal and physical threats that the children of Arab immigrants' experience have increased exponentially (Abu El-Haj, 2006; Golash-Boza, 2012; Haboush, 2007; Rong & Preissle, 2008). It is evident that the children of Arab immigrants face a number of social and political barriers and challenges within schools.

3.3 Gender

Another barrier and challenge that immigrant youth face in U.S. schools is negotiating gender roles. Oftentimes, immigrant youth must bridge the gender expectations of two different cultures – their homeland culture and U.S. culture – in the socialization and "Americanization" processes. Many immigrant youth find that their racial and ethnic identifications in the United States, as well as their English language proficiency, mark them for specific academic tracks and future career opportunities. Yet gender also plays a key role in the educational struggles that immigrant girls and boys experience in their adjustment to the United States (Kao et al., 2013; Lee, 2005, 2009; Olsen, 2008; Portes & Rumbaut, 2014; Waters, 2001).

Research studies suggest that few immigrant families are able to economically survive in the United States without both the mother and the father working outside of the home (Feliciano, 2006; Feliciano & Rumbaut, 2005; Kao et al., 2013; Olsen, 2008; Portes & Rumbaut, 2014; Rong & Preissle, 2008). As a result, female children of immigrants often assume traditional caretaker duties that include child-rearing, cooking, and cleaning. These responsibilities make it difficult for them to socialize and seek employment outside of their U.S. homes. This, in turn, leads many female children of immigrants to rely solely on education to help them realize future professional and economic success in the United States. Though it is a concern that U.S. schools place both female and male children of immigrants on low academic tracks, the effects can be more pronounced for female children of immigrants who do not have a number of paths to achievement open to them (Feliciano, 2006; Feliciano & Rumbaut, 2005; Kao et al., 2013; Olsen, 2008; Portes & Rumbaut, 2014; Rong & Preissle, 2008). In addition, many female children of immigrants report that because they dress or wear their hair differently, they are ostracized by their American peers. Without the proper support from teachers, administrators, and guidance counselors, this social isolation can lead to low self-esteem, shame, and increased depression rates the longer the female children of immigrants reside in the United States (Olsen, 2008). And, finally, it is important to point out that religion, culture, and U.S. racial stereotypes influence how female children of immigrants experience and face these challenges. The daughters of Black Caribbean, African, Latina/o, Asian, and Arab immigrants encounter and respond to these educational barriers in unique ways (Koo et al., 2012; Lee, 2005, 2009; Lee & Zhou, 2015; Peguero & Bondy, 2015; Rong & Preissle, 2008; Waters, 2001).

Gender also influences the educational challenges and barriers that male children of immigrants experience. Boys across generational, racial, and ethnic groups are more likely to be disciplined by teachers, administrators, and school security guards, less likely to be academically engaged, and more likely to report experiencing biased and unjust treatment in school than immigrant girls (Lee, 2005, 2009; Olsen, 2008; Peguero & Bondy, 2015; Rong & Preissle, 2008). Male children of immigrants' detachment from school, rather than being attributed to laziness or lack of intellectual capabilities, may be a response to the school's hostile environment (Lee, 2005, 2009; Olsen, 2008; Peguero & Bondy, 2015; Rong & Preissle, 2008). Their disengagement might thus be better understood as their attempt to deal with largely negative encounters in U.S. schools. Furthermore, because immigrant boys, unlike their female counterparts, frequently work outside of the home, they may envision paths other than school that will lead to future professional and economic success in the United States (Lee, 2005, 2009; Olsen, 2008; Peguero & Bondy, 2015; Rong & Preissle, 2008). Although most immigrant boys are aware of U.S. school and society's pervasive attitude of animosity, this insight does not improve their sense of belonging or their outcomes. Male children of immigrants who come from racial and ethnic backgrounds (e.g., Latina/o and Black Caribbean or African) that have historically been negatively stereotyped by U.S. society are especially at risk for academic detachment and failure (Lee, 2005, 2009; Olsen, 2008; Peguero & Bondy, 2015; Rong & Preissle, 2008; Waters, 2001).

3.4 English Language Proficiency

Given the numerous regions from which immigrant youth originate, it is perhaps not surprising that there are often between 20 and 100 different languages spoken by students in U.S. schools (Kao et al., 2013; Olsen, 2008; Rong & Preissle, 2008; Suárez-Orozco et al., 2009). In the midst of this linguistic diversity, educators are challenged to provide all students with the academic skills they need to succeed in life. Teachers who work to improve the educational opportunities of English language learner (ELL) students can certainly rely on the hard work, support, and high value that immigrant youth and their families place on education and learning English (Kao et al., 2013; Olsen, 2008; Rong & Preissle, 2008; Suárez-Orozco et al., 2009). Yet attention to ELL students in English as a second language programs, bilingual education programs, and language immersion programs has not resulted in advanced and consistent academic gains across grade levels and subject areas (Chudowsky & Chudowsky, 2010). Although the children of immigrants vary in their English language proficiency skills, it is important to help educators continue to understand the unique challenges and barriers that ELL students face. Not only is the number of immigrant youth in U.S. schools increasing but English language proficiency is an essential element for academic success in the United States' current English-only, high-stakes testing environment (Kao et al., 2013; Olsen, 2008; Rong & Preissle, 2008). It is thus imperative to better understand the role of the English language in the socialization and "Americanization" of the children of immigrants as they strive for educational achievement.

One theme emerging from the research on ELL students in the United States is that curriculum and pedagogy, especially when it is Eurocentric and English only, minimizes the language, identity, and culture of immigrant youth. Research demonstrates that when schools adopt policies and practices that attempt to linguistically and culturally assimilate ELL students into dominant U.S. society, lower self-esteem, higher depression rates, and detachment from school often result (Kao et al., 2013; Olsen, 2008; Rong & Preissle, 2008; Suárez-Orozco et al., 2009). In addition, while teachers and administrators do not explicitly state that they think ELL students are not as intelligent as their U.S.-born peers, their behavior toward and treatment of ELL students can suggest otherwise. Schools often use approaches that are not content-based (e.g., worksheets about holidays, food, and customs) and that do not take into consideration ELL students' ages or previous educational experiences (Kao et al., 2013; Olsen, 2008; Rong & Preissle, 2008; Suárez-Orozco et al., 2009). Perhaps because teachers and administrators often do not have the time to explore the current research regarding bilingual and bicultural development, they continue to use curricular and pedagogical practices that lack both academic rigor and appreciation for ELL students' linguistic and cultural diversity.

A second theme emerging from the research on ELL students in U.S. schools is the mainstream perception of their spoken English. Although all people who speak English speak it with one accent or another, ELL students who speak English with an accent tend to experience negative feedback from their teachers and peers. ELL students report being patronized by and receiving lower grades from their teachers because of their English-speaking accents and skills (Kao et al., 2013; Olsen, 2008; Rong & Preissle, 2008; Suárez-Orozco et al., 2009). It is possible that teachers' lack of knowledge about second-language acquisition and second-language literacy development can unintentionally result in lower grades and unique educational barriers and challenges for ELL students. There is also research that describes situations in school where ELL students are verbally and physically harassed by their U.S.-born peers who claim to not understand their spoken English (Kao et al., 2013; Olsen, 2008; Rong & Preissle, 2008; Suárez-Orozco et al., 2009). Perceptions of ELL students' English-speaking competencies restrict their access to American culture by creating obstacles to "fitting in" with and talking to U.S.-born students. Negative feedback from teachers and peers bar ELL students from the kinds of interactions that would help them attain a more advanced level of academic knowledge, acquire a greater level of English proficiency, and develop a sense of themselves as valued members of the United States (Kao et al., 2013; Lee, 2005, 2009; Olsen, 2008; Rong & Preissle, 2008; Suárez-Orozco et al., 2009). As Creese and Kambere (2003) note, language and accents are not about communication; rather, they are about "power and exclusion, marginalization and 'Othering,' racism and discrimination" (p. 571). In other words, English-speaking accents and skills can draw a distinction between youth who are and who are not perceived as academically, socially, and culturally competent in U.S. schools.

3.5 Family

Immigrants and their children generally come to the United States with high aspirations and a strong work ethic to pursue the *globalized* phenomenon of the "American Dream" (Kasinitz et al., 2009; Louie, 2012; Portes & Rumbaut, 2014). Ideally, these values should help insulate the children of immigrants from various negative influences in U.S. society, but they are not always sufficient to keep children on pathways to educational success over time. Upon arrival, immigrants and their children are confronted with the reality of inequality, biased treatment, and stratification in U.S. schools (Kao et al., 2013; Louie, 2012; Olsen, 2008; Portes & Rumbaut, 2014; Rong & Preissle, 2008; Waters, 2001). Because it is well-known that family characteristics (e.g., family socioeconomic status, parental education, and health, stability) are foundational for educational progress, it is imperative to understand these considerations when assessing the educational potential and success of students within U.S. schools.

Unfortunately, many immigrant families often face and encounter a significant number of social, economic, and cultural barriers and hurdles that marginalize immigrants and their children. Immigrant parents are more likely to live in poverty and social isolation, experience emotional depression due to acculturation stress, lack health insurance,

and even have educational degrees and accreditations that are not rec-
ognized or acknowledged (Kao et al., 2013; Louie, 2012; Olsen, 2008;
Portes & Rumbaut, 2014; Rong & Preissle, 2008; Suárez-Orozco
et al., 2009; Waters, 2001). As a result, the children of immigrants self-
impose a significant amount of pressure to do well in school because of
a sense of obligation or responsibility to repay their immigrant parents
for the sacrifices the parents made to come to the United States, as
well as a desire to obtain well-paying jobs to help support their families
in the future (Lee & Zhou, 2015; Louie, 2012; Portes & Rumbaut,
2014). Even though the children of immigrants are incredibly motivated to do well in school, immigrant parents are often restricted from
facilitating effective navigation of their children through an unfamiliar
and complex school system. This phenomenon is exemplified within
the educational conceptualization of parental involvement.

Although there are a number of ways that parental involvement can
facilitate educational progress for children, we will highlight two major
obstacles that immigrant parents face in relation to parental involvement. First, parental involvement should provide parents with a means
of social control because involved parents get to know other parents,
teachers, and administrators who may then discuss their children's performance effectively with them. Research reveals, however, that teachers, school administrators, and other parents do not approach immigrant
parents because of language barriers, xenophobia, and bias (Kao et al.,
2013; Lee, 2005, 2009; Rong & Preissle, 2008; Turney & Kao, 2009).
Second, involved parents are privy to information about their children
because teachers tell parents that their children are struggling in order to
intervene. Meanwhile, studies have shown that immigrant parents are
often not contacted by school officials, nor can they effectively contact
the school because translators are not available or offered (Kao et al.,
2013; Lee, 2005, 2009; Rong & Preissle, 2008; Turney & Kao, 2009).

3.6 Documentation Status

There is limited research about the violence and safety problems that
undocumented youth experience specifically in U.S. schools. Considering the current socio-political context discussed in Chapter 2,
more research on the school experiences of undocumented youth is
warranted and needed. With this noted, we shall generally discuss the
research about how violence and safety are part of undocumented
youth's daily lives. Estimates indicate that over two million undocumented youth are enrolled in U.S. public schools (Passel & Cohn, 2009)
and approximately 3.9 million students have at least one unauthorized

parent (Passel & Cohn, 2016). Yet 30 years after the landmark con-
stitutional decision *Plyler vs. Doe* (1982) gave undocumented children
the legal right to a pre-K–12 education, they remain one of the most
vulnerable populations in the educational system. Less than 40 percent of undocumented youth between the ages of 18 and 24 graduate from high school, a rate significantly higher than documented
immigrants (15 percent) and U.S.-born residents (8 percent) (Passel &
Cohn, 2016). In the context of heated national debates about immigration and immigration reform, the outcome of *Plyler vs. Doe* (1982)
calls for attention. This section highlights the immigration laws, policies, and practices that impact undocumented youth in U.S. public
schools. More specifically, we pay particular attention to how law- and
policymaking around immigration are associated with violence, victimization, and safety for the children of immigrants in schools. We
conclude by exploring some of the educational implications.

In discussing the vulnerabilities associated with the children of immigrants, as well as how to move forward with thinking about school safety,
we would first like to make explicit the assumption from which we are
working. As numerous scholars point out, undocumented youth's school
experiences must be studied in relation to how they converge with the
implementation of immigration and criminal law (Dabach, 2015; Gallo,
2014; Gallo & Link, 2015; Gonzales, 2016; Jeffries & Dabach, 2015;
Menjívar & Abrego, 2012a, 2012b; Patel, 2013). At the same time that
undocumented youth are guaranteed legal access to pre-K–12 educational institutions, national and state immigration policies and enforcement have shifted and intensified to their detriment over the last several
years. In what follows, we briefly describe federal and national changes
in immigration policy. Our time line begins in the mid-1990s and ends
with the current presidential administration in 2016. Our goal is to demonstrate that immigration enforcement and xenophobia are not new phenomena; rather, spoken and unspoken attitudes toward immigration have
become increasingly polarized since Donald Trump took office in 2016.

At the federal level, there have been several shifts in immigration
policy over the past three decades. Under the Clinton administration in the 1990s, the Illegal Immigration Reform and Responsibility
Act of 1996 not only expanded the bases on which undocumented
immigrants could be deported, but it also restricted their access to
public and social benefits. Additionally, under the Bush administration
in the early 2000s, the 2003 transfer of Immigration and Naturaliza-
tion Service duties to the Department of Homeland Security further
criminalized immigration and added another layer to immigration

imprisonment (Bosworth & Kaufman, 2011). Then under the Obama administration, the Priority Enforcement Program (2014), similar to its predecessor, the Secure Communities program (2008–2014), checked the fingerprints of people booked into local and state custody, "regardless of whether they have been formally charged, tried, and convicted of any crime" (ACLU, 2014, p. 1). There was also a growing focus on the removal of undocumented immigrants, and the number of deportations rose to 438,421 in the fiscal year 2013 (USDHS, 2013). These initiatives, along with the strengthening of Immigration and Customs Enforcement (ICE) and Customs and Border Patrol, add layers of complexity to U.S. immigration enforcement.

K–12 immigrant and undocumented students are vulnerable to shifts in federal immigration policy. Partly to remove immigration enforcement attention away from individuals with good behavior, President Obama also initiated the Deferred Actions for Childhood Arrivals (DACA) in 2012. DACA allowed some undocumented immigrants brought into the United States at a young age a two-year renewable period of reprieve from deportation and eligibility to pursue a work permit and higher education. DACA recipients could apply for Social Security numbers and driver's licenses, thus facilitating their integration into U.S. society. While DACA remains an imperfect policy, it did create freedom and independence for undocumented students and enabled them to pursue a brighter future (Chávez, Monforti, & Michelson, 2014; Gonzales et al., 2014). However, when Donald Trump took office, immigration policy changed again.

Since his election in 2016, Trump's immigration agenda has been expansive. Not only has the administration broadened the discretion of immigration enforcement officers to detain undocumented immigrants for lengths of time far beyond those who have committed crimes, but it has also attempted to repeal DACA. Furthermore, the Trump administration has enforced a zero-tolerance policy that separates children from their families at the border, including those families who are asylum seekers and legally present themselves at checkpoints (Cleek, 2018). While Trump has replaced approximately 400 miles of pre-existing wall along the U.S./Mexico border, questions remain about whether his administration will follow through with promises to build a wall along the entirety of the border (Merchant, 2020). The DACA repeal, coupled with heightened immigration enforcement, has had a chilling effect on students, families, and schools (Andrade, 2019b; Wray-Lake et al., 2018). When such virulent anti-immigrant sentiment seeps into schools, the political tensions can be devastating for students whose academic and social success depends greatly on favorable school contexts (Andrade, 2019a, 2019b; Murillo, 2017; Pérez, 2012).

Along with these federal efforts since the mid-1990s, some states have passed and/or repealed their own educational and immigration laws. Between 1998 and 2003, California, Arizona, and Massachusetts passed English-only educational policies, essentially abolishing bilingual education in public schools. Research documents the harmful effects on the socio-emotional and academic development of children of immigrants who are ELL students, as well as how these laws exacerbate racial and linguistic segregation in schools (Bondy, 2011, 2016; Cammarota & Aguilera, 2012; Gándara & Orfield, 2012). Although California and Massachusetts have since repealed their English-only educational policies and reinstated bilingual education, the effect of this reimplementation on students has been fragmented within and across school districts and is not yet well documented. In 2010, Arizona passed SB 1070, which permitted law enforcement to, in effect, curtail due process and question the immigration status of anyone detained for a minor infraction (Arrocha, 2012). Similar legislation to this policy also passed in 2011 in both Georgia (HB 87) and Alabama (HB 56) (Arrocha, 2012). The conjoining of federal and state policies around immigration arguably marginalizes undocumented immigrants. Such immigration policies also potentially create a fearful and hostile environment that presents particular barriers for undocumented youth in U.S. schools. This fear and hostility, whether real or perceived, harms the children of immigrants' socialization and incorporation processes in U.S. schools.

Schools should provide a stable and safe haven for all students, regardless of documentation status. However, despite efforts by some school personnel to keep children safe and despite *Plyler vs. Doe's* (1982) legal guarantee to pre-K–12 educational access, many undocumented youth report feeling unsafe and unwelcome in school environments. For example, although these kinds of searches have been prohibited, ICE agents in Detroit followed undocumented Latino parents from their homes as they brought their children to school, detaining the parents within view of others (News America Media, 2011). ICE agents in Los Angeles also arrested a father after he dropped off one of his daughters at school. The father's second daughter was in the car when ICE detained him (Sanchez, 2017). Additionally, shortly after Arizona SB 1070, Georgia HB 87, and Alabama HB 56 went into effect, thousands of schoolchildren were reported absent, and immigrants began to confine themselves to their homes, fearful of leaving (Arrocha, 2012). Similarly, after the Trump administration ramped up ICE workplace raids in states such as Ohio and Mississippi, separating children from their parents, reports abounded of children's depression, anxiety, and isolation (Saslow, 2018). Fear of deportation and family separation keep many undocumented youth from sharing their documentation status with teachers and other school personnel, who have the power to report their family's status to immigration authorities (Abrego, 2008; Jeffries & Dabach, 2015; Patel, 2013; Pérez, 2012). Fear of deportation and family separation also contribute to undocumented youth's increased risk of depression and anxiety and stress related to racial and xenophobic discrimination in schools (APA, 2012).

There is a small but growing number of studies describing the relationships between undocumented youth and pre-K–12 school authorities and peers. Some of these studies conclude that undocumented youth, particularly those who attend schools with higher percentages of undocumented students and are enrolled in smaller honors and advanced placement classes, have largely positive interactions with teachers, counselors, and administrators (Enriquez, 2011; Gonzales, 2010; Gonzales, Heredia, & Negrón-Gonzales, 2015; Nienhusser, Vega, & Saavedra Carquin, 2016; Patel, 2013). However, these investigations also find negative experiences, such as perceptions of low academic ability, enrollment in large general and remedial education classes, and insensitive jokes about immigration status exhibited by high school personnel toward undocumented students (Andrade, 2019a; Enriquez, 2011; Gonzales, 2010; Gonzales et al., 2015; Nienhusser et al., 2016; Patel, 2013). Undocumented youth also report concerns about being stigmatized by peers if their documentation status is revealed (Abrego, 2008; Jeffries & Dabach, 2015; Patel, 2013; Pérez, 2012). Fear of authorities, perceptions of low academic abilities, and stress of stigmatization create obstacles to incorporation and mobility in the United States and hinder undocumented youth's sense of belonging.

Additionally, although *Plyler vs. Doe* (1982) guarantees undocumented youth legal access to pre-K–12 educational institutions, nothing guarantees access to higher education. Many undocumented students in high school report being high achievers and college bound (Abrego, 2008; Abrego & Gonzales, 2010; Gonzales, 2011; Menjívar & Abrego, 2012a, 2012b). However, once learning that their documentation status bars them from either in-state college tuition or financial aid, many youth cease to excel in school and experience diminishing academic motivation and aspirations (Abrego, 2008; Abrego & Gonzales, 2010; Gonzales, 2011; Menjívar & Abrego, 2012a, 2012b). Undocumented youth are socialized in the U.S. to have legal access to schools and to develop a strong sense of belonging and belief in the American Dream.

In terms of moving forward in thinking about school safety and undocumented youth, there are at least three emergent areas of focus. First, during heightened immigration enforcement and deportation threats, undocumented youth may be fearful of detainment of themselves or a family member, as well as fearful of family separation. Undocumented youth may also face classrooms where their presence is invalidated or made the subject of mockery by teachers and peers. Therefore, we see a need for research that explores classroom and school climates that protect and nourish undocumented youth's emotional safety. Second, an important tension arises when undocumented youth approach high school graduation and seek to attend college. While teachers may not be financial aid experts, school counselors provide valuable information regarding the college and financial aid application processes. Future research can explore how staff members are educated on the college choice and financial aid processes, as well as how schools can connect with community resources and local advocacy groups to help undocumented students develop a network and navigate access to higher education so that they may experience more opportunities for economic mobility. Finally, at the time of revising this chapter, the United States just elected its forty-sixth president, Joseph R. Biden. President-Elect Biden has already promised to fully reinstate DACA and halt Trump's travel and immigration restrictions on 13 countries. As immigration policies once again shift across presidential administrations, issues surrounding school safety and documentation status will continue to be a pressing concern. Preparing researchers and practitioners to understand these shifts and engage with immigration policy will allow news forums and spaces that in turn increase school safety for all youth.

In this chapter, we presented the intersecting factors associated with immigration and school safety. We showed how exposure to violence and victimization at school is disparate across distinct segments of the student population, especially for the children of immigrants. We also illustrated that the population of children of immigrants attending U.S. schools is diverse. The research evidence highlighted in this chapter demonstrates the inequalities and disparities associated with the population of children of immigrants in terms of their school safety. It is clear that if faculty, staff, practitioners, and policymakers are to pursue ways to ameliorate the vulnerabilities to violence and victimization for the children of immigrants, it is fundamental to consider factors such as race, ethnicity, region of origin, gender, English language proficiency, family, and documentation status in association with school violence and safety.

References

Abrego, L. J. (2008). Legitimacy, social identity, and the mobilization of law: The effects of assembly bill 540 on undocumented students in California. *Law & Social Inquiry, 33*(3), 709–734.

Abrego, L. J., & Gonzales, R. G. (2010). Blocked paths, uncertain futures: The postsecondary education and labor market prospects of undocumented Latino youth. *Journal of Education for Students Placed at Risk, 15*, 144–157.

Abu El-Haj, T. R. (2006). Race, politics, and Arab American youth: Shifting frameworks for conceptualizing educational equity. *Educational Policy, 20*, 13–34.

American Civil Liberties Union. (2014). *DHS secretary Johnson discontinues secure communities "as we know it."* Retrieved from www.aclu.org/sites/default/files/field_document/2014_12_18_-_aclu_summary_of_dhs_scomm_and_detainer_reforms_final.pdf

American Psychological Association. (2012). *Crossroads: The psychology of immigration in the new century.* Washington, DC: American Psychological Association.

Andrade, L. M. (2019a). "The war still continues": The importance of positive validation for undocumented students one year after Trump's presidential victory. *Journal of Hispanic Higher Education, 18*(3), 273–289.

Andrade, L. M. (2019b). "The war still continues," part II: The importance of positive validation for undocumented students one year after Trump's presidential victory. *Journal of Hispanic Higher Education, 17*(4).

Apple, M., & Franklin, B. (2004). Curricular history and social control. In M. Apple (Ed.), *Ideology and curriculum* (pp. 59–76). New York: Routledge Falmer.

Arrocha, W. (2012). From Arizona's S.B. 1070 to Georgia's H.B. 87 and Alabama's H.B. 56: Exacerbating the other and generating new discourses and practices of segregation. *California Western Law Review, 48*(2), 245–278.

Bondy, J. M. (2011). Normalizing English language learner students: A Foucauldian analysis of opposition to bilingual education. *Race, Ethnicity and Education, 14*(3), 387–398.

Bondy, J. M. (2016). Latina youth, education, and citizenship: A feminist transnational analysis. *Theory & Research in Social Education, 44*(2), 212–243.

Bosworth, M., & Kaufman, E. (2011). Foreigners in a carceral age: Immigration and imprisonment in the United States. *Stanford Law & Policy Review, 22*(2), 429–454.

Brunson, R., & Miller, J. (2009). Schools, neighborhoods, and adolescent conflicts: A situational examination of reciprocal dynamics. *Justice Quarterly, 26*, 183–210.

Cammarota, J., & Aguilera, M. (2012). "By the time I get to Arizona": Race, language, and education in America's racist state. *Race, Ethnicity & Education, 15*(4), 485–500.

Chávez, M., Monforti, J. L. L., & Michelson, M. R. (2014). *Living the dream: New immigration policies and the lives of undocumented Latino youth.* Boulder, CO: Paradigm.

Chudowsky, N., & Chudowsky, V. (2010). *State test score trends through 2007–08, part 6: Has progress been made in raising achievement for English language learners?* Washington, DC: Center on Education Policy.

Cleek, A. (2018, June 6). For this mother and daughter, separated a year ago at the Southern border, Trump's "zero-tolerance" policy isn't new. *Public Radio International*. Retrieved from www.pri.org/stories/2018-06-06/mother-and-daughter-separated-year-ago- southernborder-trumps-zero-tolerance

Creese, G., & Kambere, E. N. (2003). What colour is your English? *Canadian Review of Sociology and Anthropology, 40*(5), 565–573.

Crenshaw, K. (1990). Mapping the margins: Intersectionality, identity politics, and violence against women of color. *Stanford Law Review, 43*, 1241–1299.

Dabach, D. B. (2015). Teacher placement into immigrant English learner classrooms: Limiting access in comprehensive high schools. *American Educational Research Journal, 52*, 243–274.

Dettlaff, A. J., Earner, I., & Phillips, S. D. (2009). Latino children of immigrants in the child welfare system: Prevalence, characteristics, and risk. *Children and Youth Services Review, 31*(7), 775–783.

Enriquez, L. E. (2011). "Because we feel the pressure, we also feel the support": Examining educational success of undocumented immigrant Latino/s students. *Harvard Educational Review, 81*(3), 476–499.

Feliciano, C. (2006). *Unequal origins: Immigrant selection and the education of the second generation.* New York: LFB Scholarly Publishing.

Feliciano, C., & Rumbaut, R. (2005). Gendered paths: Educational and occupational expectations and outcomes among adult children of immigrants. *Ethnic and Racial Studies, 28*, 1087–1118.

Gallo, S. (2014). The effects of gendered immigration enforcement on middle childhood and schooling. *American Educational Research Journal, 51*(3), 473–504.

Gallo, S., & Link, H. (2015). "Diles la verdad": Deportation policies, politicized funds of knowledge, and schooling in middle childhood. *Harvard Educational Review, 85*(3), 357–382.

Gándara, P., & Orfield, G. (2012). Segregating Arizona's English learners: A return to the "Mexican room"? *Teachers College Record, 114*(9), 1–27.

Golash-Boza, T. (2012). *Immigration nation: Raids, detentions, and deportations in post–9/11 America.* Boulder, CO: Paradigm.

Gonzales, R. G. (2010). On the wrong side of the tracks: Understanding the effects of school structure and social capital in the educational pursuits of undocumented immigrant students. *Peabody Journal of Education, 85*(4), 469–485.

Gonzales, R. G. (2011). Learning to be illegal: Undocumented youth and shifting legal contexts in the transition to adulthood. *American Sociological Review, 76*, 602–619.

Gonzales, R. G. (2016). *Lives in limbo: Undocumented and coming of age in America.* Berkeley, CA: University of California Press.

Gonzales, R. G., Heredia, L. L., & Negrón-Gonzales, G. N. (2015). Untangling Plyler's legacy: Undocumented students, schools, and citizenship. *Harvard Educational Review, 85*(3), 318–341.

Gonzales, R.G., Terriquez, V., & Ruszczyk, S. P. (2014). Becoming DACA-mented: Assessing the short-term benefits of deferred action for childhood arrivals (DACA). *American Behavioral Scientist, 58*(14), 1852–1872.

Gottfredson, D. C. (2001). *Schools and delinquency.* New York: Cambridge University Press.

Haboush, K. L. (2007). Working with Arab American families: Culturally competent practice for school psychologists. *Psychology in the Schools, 44*, 183–198.

Hong, J. S. (2009). Feasibility of the Olweus bullying prevention program in low-income schools. *Journal of School Violence, 8*, 81–97.

Hong, J. S., Merrin, G. J., Peguero, A. A., Gonzalez-Prendes, A. A., & Lee, N. Y. (2016). Exploring the social-ecological determinants of physical fighting in U.S. schools: What about youth in immigrant families? *Child & Youth Care Forum, 45*(2), 279–299.

Hong, J. S., Peguero, A. A., Choi, S., Lanesskog, D., Espelage, D., & Lee, N. Y. (2014). School bullying and peer victimization of Latino and Asian American youth: A social-ecological framework. *Journal of School Violence, 13*, 315–338.

Jeffries, J., & Dabach, D. B. (2015). Breaking the silence: Facing undocumented issues in teacher practice. *Association of Mexican-American Educators Journal, 8*(1), 83–93.

Kao, G., Vaquera, E., & Goyette, K. (2013). *Education and immigration.* Malden, MA: Policy Press.

Kasinitz, P., Mollenkopf, J.H., Waters, M.C., & Holdaway, J. (2009). *Inheriting the city: The children of immigrants come of age.* New York: Russell Sage Foundation.

Koch, J. M. (2007). How schools can best support Somali students and their families. *International Journal of Multicultural Education, 9*(1), 1–15.

Koo, D. J., Peguero, A. A., & Shekarkhar, Z. (2012). The "model minority" victim: Immigration, gender, and Asian American vulnerabilities to violence at school." *Journal of Ethnicity in Criminal Justice, 10*, 129–147.

Kumi-Yeboah, A., Brobbey, G., & Smith, P. (2020). Exploring factors that facilitate acculturation strategies and academic success of West African immigrant youth in urban schools. *Education and Urban Society, 52*(1), 21–50.

Lee, S. J. (2005). *Up against Whiteness: Race, school and immigrant youth.* New York: Teachers College Press.

Lee, S. J. (2009). *Unraveling the model minority stereotype: Listening to Asian American youth.* New York: Teachers College Press.

Lee, S. J., & Zhou, M. (2015). *The Asian American achievement paradox.* New York: Russell Sage Foundation.

Lewis, A. E., & Diamond, J. B. (2015). *Despite the best intentions: How racial inequality thrives in good schools.* Oxford: Oxford University Press.

Louie, V. (2012). *Keeping the immigrant bargain: The costs and rewards of success in America.* New York: Russell Sage Foundation.

Merchant, N. (29 October 2020). Trump officials tout progress on border wall before elections. Retrieved from: https://apnews.com/article/donald-trump-virus-outbreak-wildlife-mexico-fencing-07406460e33303726fa9bed9594c21ff

Menjívar, C., & Abrego, L. J. (2012a). Legal violence: Immigration law and the lives of Central American immigrants. *The American Journal of Sociology, 117*, 1380–1421.

Menjívar, C., & Abrego, L. (2012b). *Legal violence in the lives of immigrants: How immigration enforcement affects families, schools, and workplaces.* Center for American Progress. Retrieved from https://cdn.americanprogress.org/wp-content/uploads/2012/12/MenjivarLegalViolenceReport.pdf

Morenoff, J. D., Sampson, R. J., & Raudenbush, S. W. (2001). Neighborhood inequality, collective efficacy, and the spatial dynamics of urban violence. *Criminology, 39*(3), 517–558.

Morris, M. W. (2016). *Pushout: The criminalization of Black girls in schools.* New York: The New Press.

Murillo, M. A. (2017). The art of the reveal: Undocumented high school students, institutional agents, and the disclosure of legal status. *The High School Journal, 100*(2), 88–108.

News America Media. (8 April 2011). *ICE stalks immigrant parents at Detroit school.* Retrieved from: http://newamericamedia.org/2011/04/ice-stalks-immigrant-parents-at-detroit-school.php

Nienhusser, H. K., Vega, B. E., & Saavedra Carquin, M. C. (2016). Undocumented students' experiences with microaggressions during their college choice process. *Teachers College Record, 118*, 1–34.

Noguera, P. A. (2009). *The trouble with Black boys: And other reflections on race, equity, and the future of public education.* San Francisco, CA: Jossey-Bass.

Olsen, L. (2008). *Made in America: Immigrant students in our public schools.* New York: New York University Press.

Passel, J. S., & Cohn, D. (2009). *A portrait of unauthorized immigrants in the United States.* Pew Hispanic Center. Retrieved from www.pewhispanic.org/files/reports/107.pdf

Passel, J. S., & Cohn, D. (2016, November 17). *Children of unauthorized immigrants represent rising share of K-12 students.* Retrieved from www.pewresearch.org/fact-tank/2016/11/17/children-of-unauthorized-immigrants-represent-rising-share-of-k-12-students/

Patel, L. (2013). *Youth held at the border: Immigration, education, and the politics of inclusion.* New York: Teachers College Press.

Peguero, A. A. (2009). Victimizing the children of immigrants: Latino and Asian American student victimization. *Youth & Society, 41*, 186–208.

Peguero, A. A. (2011). Immigration, schools, and violence: Assimilation and student misbehavior. *Sociological Spectrum, 31*, 695–717.

Peguero, A. A. (2012). Schools, bullying, and inequality: Intersecting factors and complexities with the stratification of youth victimization at school. *Sociology Compass, 6*, 402–412.

Peguero, A. A. (2013). An adolescent victimization immigrant paradox?: School-based routines, lifestyles, and victimization across immigration generations. *Journal of Youth and Adolescence, 42*, 1759–1773.

Peguero, A. A., & Bondy, J. M. (2015). Schools, justice, and immigrant students: Assimilation, race, ethnicity, gender, and perceptions of fairness and order. *Teachers College Record, 117*, 1–42.

Peguero, A. A., & Jiang, X. (2014). Social control across immigrant generations: Adolescent violence at school and examining the immigrant paradox. *Journal of Criminal Justice, 42*(3), 276–287.

Peguero, A. A., & Popp, A. M. (2012). Youth violence at school and the intersection of gender, race, and ethnicity. *Journal of Criminal Justice, 40*(1), 1–9.

Peguero, A. A., & Shekarkhar, Z. (2011). Latino/a student misbehavior and school punishment. *Hispanic Journal of Behavioral Sciences, 33*(1), 54–70.

Pérez, W. (2012). *Americans by heart.* New York: Teachers College Press.

Portes, A., & Rumbaut, R. (2014). *Immigrant America: A portrait.* Berkeley, CA: University of California Press.

Potter, H. (2015). *Intersectionality and criminology: Disrupting and revolutionizing studies of crime.* London: Routledge Falmer.

Rojas-Gaona, C. E., Hong, J. S., & Peguero, A. A. (2016). The significance of race/ethnicity in adolescent violence: A decade of review, 2005–2015. *Journal of Criminal Justice, 46*, 137–147.

Rong, X., & Preissle, J. (2008). *Educating immigrant students in the 21st century: What we need to know to meet the challenges.* Thousand Oaks, CA: Corwin Press.

Sampson, R. J., & Sharkey, P. (2008). Neighborhood selection and the social reproduction of concentrated racial inequality. *Demography, 45*(1), 1–29.

Sanchez, R. (3 March 2017). *ICE arrests undocumented father taking daughter to California school.* Retrieved from: https://www.cnn.com/2017/03/03/us/california-father-ice-arrest-trnd/index.html

Saslow, E. (2018, June 30). "Are you alone now?": After raid, immigrant families are separated in America's heartland. *The Washington Post.* Retrieved from www.washington post.com/news/national/wp/2018/06/30/feature/are-you-alone-now-after-raid-immigrant-families-are-separated-in-the-american-heartland/?utm_term=.ae64abefe743

Suárez-Orozco, C., Suárez-Orozco, M., & Todorova, I. (2009). *Learning a new land: Immigrant students in American society.* Cambridge, MA: Harvard University Press.

Turney, K., & Kao, G. (2009). Barriers to school involvement: Are immigrant parents disadvantaged? *The Journal of Educational Research, 102*, 257–271.

United States Census Bureau. (2017). *Current population survey.* Washington, DC: United States Census Bureau, Population Division.

United States Department of Homeland Security (USDHS). (2013). *Yearbook of immigration statistics: 2013 enforcement actions.* Retrieved from: https://www.ice.gov/removal-statistics

Waters, M. (2001). *Black identities: West Indian immigrant dreams and American realities.* Boston, MA: Harvard University Press.

Wray-Lake, L., Wells, R., Alvis, L., Delgado, S., Syversten, A. K., & Metzger, A. (2018). Being a Latinx adolescent under a Trump presidency: Analysis of Latinx youth's reactions to immigration politics. *Children and Youth Services Review, 87*, 192–204.

Chapter 4

The Significance of Criminology Theories

In this chapter, we argue that researchers, policymakers, and community stakeholders who are pursuing evidence-based efforts toward ensuring safety for all students should incorporate criminology theories to understand and address the relationships between immigration and school safety. It is clear that there is a school violence "immigrant paradox" occurring within U.S. schools that warrants discussion. This paradox has also fueled criminological investigation to understand this phenomenon; however, only a limited number of studies have investigated the role of immigration to understand and address school violence, as well as ensure safety for the children of immigrants. We highlight five theoretical approaches that are often utilized to address school violence, as well as pursue safety for students: 1) social-ecology, 2) social bonds, 3) opportunity, 4) minority threat, and 5) procedural justice. We also underscore research evidence that clearly suggests immigration is important to consider within the tenets of these theories. We summarize research findings that denote how the utilization of these theories can explain the children of immigrants' engagement in offending and vulnerability to violence and victimization in order to help ensure safety and improve educational experiences; however, the need to further draw upon criminology theories for future research about immigration and school safety is made evident here.

4.1 The School Violence "Immigrant Paradox"

As noted throughout this chapter, a growing number of researchers have examined how the children of immigrants are adapting to U.S. culture and society. What is emerging from this research is a phenomenon called the "immigrant paradox" – the counterintuitive finding that adapting to U.S. cultural and social norms may be resulting in detrimental outcomes. Studies reveal that assimilation for immigrants and their children is associated with increased psychological and health problems, educational failure, deviant behavior, drug use, and violence, such as victimization and engagement in delinquent and criminal behavior (Bui, 2015; Desmond & Kubrin, 2009; DiPietro & McGloin, 2012; DiPietro, Slocum, & Esbensen, 2015; Kubrin & Desmond, 2015; Miller & Peguero, 2018; Peguero & Hong, 2019; Portes & Rumbaut, 2014; Rengifo & Fratello, 2015; Wright & Rodriguez, 2014).

The National Longitudinal Study of Adolescent Health (Add Health) incorporates a primary sampling frame that is stratified (by region of the country, urbanicity, percentage White, size, and school type). Add Health also consists of a sample of 80 high schools, which were selected with unequal probability. Fifty-two middle schools that supplied students to the high schools were also included in the sample, for a total of 132 schools. In addition to these surveys, the Add Health data contain numerous contextual variables, most taken from the 1990 Census of Population and Housing, which Add Health researchers linked to respondents' identification numbers. The contextual data supply information on the neighborhood context in which adolescents reside. A number of studies analyzed this data to explore the adolescent violent immigrant paradox. Desmond and Kubrin (2009) found that, although neighborhood immigrant concentration is negatively related to adolescent violence, the protective effects of immigrant concentration are stronger for some types of youth than others, with Asian youth reaping the greatest benefits. Kubrin and Desmond (2015) revealed that social capital and personal and vicarious victimization do not mediate the relationship between neighborhood immigrant concentration and adolescent violence. Jiang and Peterson (2012) found that while third-plus generation youth benefited from participation in extracurricular activities, for both first- and second-generation immigrant adolescents, participation was associated with an increased likelihood of violence, challenging the broad assumption that such activities are necessarily beneficial for all youth.

It is argued that many immigrant parents, as well as their immigrant children, are socialized with native cultural beliefs of respecting authority (e.g., parents, teachers) and being obedient; on the other hand, native-born *or* third-plus-generation youth have more engagement in deviance and criminal activity (Bui, 2009, 2015; Desmond & Kubrin, 2009; DiPietro & McGloin, 2012; Kubrin & Desmond,

2015; Portes & Rumbaut, 2014; Wright & Rodriguez, 2014). Moreover, first-generation immigrants have optimistic attitudes about upward mobility for themselves, as well as their children; however, that optimism tends to erode by the third-plus generation due to racism, biased treatment, and blocked opportunities (Bui, 2009, 2015; Desmond & Kubrin, 2009; DiPietro & McGloin, 2012; Kubrin & Desmond, 2015; Miller & Peguero, 2018; Portes & Rumbaut, 2014; Rengifo & Fratello, 2015; Sampson, 2008). Contact with deviant youth increases engagement in deviance for the children of immigrants (Bui, 2009, 2015; Desmond & Kubrin, 2009; DiPietro & McGloin, 2012; Kubrin & Desmond, 2015; Portes & Rumbaut, 2014; Sampson, 2008). The process of becoming American is presumed to be one of becoming deviant – that is, assimilating the American phenomenon and tradition of a "moral rejection of authority" (Zhou, 1997). Also, studies find that the proportion of immigrant residents and social and physical disorder are associated with engagement in violence and deviance, as well as victimization for the children of immigrants. A higher proportion of immigrants within a community is associated with a reduction of youth engagement in deviance and victimization (Bui, 2009, 2015; Desmond & Kubrin, 2009; DiPietro & McGloin, 2012; Kubrin & Desmond, 2015; Portes & Rumbaut, 2014; Sampson, 2008). Social disorder (e.g., high population of deviant youth, culture of deviance, gang prevalence) and physical disorder (e.g., graffiti, litter, deteriorating buildings) may be contextual factors that contribute to youth violence and deviance within immigrant communities (Bui, 2009, 2015; Desmond & Kubrin, 2009; Kubrin & Desmond, 2015; Portes & Rumbaut, 2014; Sampson, 2008). This pattern of the immigrant paradox with violence is also being found within schools.

Some suggest that there is a school violence "immigrant paradox" occurring in the U.S. educational system. As the children of immigrants assimilate, so does their likelihood of engaging in disrespectful attitudes and other misconduct, being victimized, and being punished (DiPietro et al., 2015; Hong et al., 2014; Hong, Merrin, Peguero, Gonzalez-Prendes, & Lee, 2016; Peguero, 2009, 2011, 2012a, 2013; Peguero & Bondy, 2015; Watkins & Melde, 2009). The Educational Longitudinal Study (ELS) of 2002 is a longitudinal survey administered by the Research Triangle Institute for the National Center for Education Statistics of the U.S. Department of Education. ELS is designed to monitor the transition of a national sample of young people as they progress from tenth grade through high school and on to postsecondary education and/or the world of work. A number of research studies exploring the children of immigrants' school experiences draw from ELS for a subsample consisting of 9,870 children of immigrants in 580 public schools. There are three multilevel ELS studies that exemplify the barriers and hurdles that reflect a school violence immigrant paradox. Peguero (2011) finds that first-generation immigrants are less likely to engage in school-based misbehaviors, such as cutting class and getting into fights, than their U.S. native-born counterparts. Peguero and Jiang (2014) suggest the counterintuitive finding that extracurricular involvement in school-based activities contributes to the children of immigrants' school-based misbehavior and victimization. Peguero, Shekarkhar, Popp, and Koo (2015) indicate that even though the children of immigrants are less likely to engage in school-based misbehavior, they experience the increased likelihood of being punished at school. Thus, since there is evidence of a school violence immigrant paradox occurring, as well as knowledge of the vulnerability that the children of immigrants face while at school, a body of research is emerging that draws on criminology theories to investigate, understand, and address the relationship between immigration and school violence.

4.2 The Importance of Criminology Theories

There is an established trend of a "school as community" approach toward investigating school violence and safety. Schools are fundamentally a community because they reflect many of the social mechanisms, bureaucracy, shared cultural values (i.e., focus on education), and behavioral patterns that are represented within communities. As in communities, school participants (i.e., faculty, students, staff, and administrators) share common activities, routines, and symbiotic interactions that influence one another and an ethos of caring that ideally connects all school participants (Gottfredson, 2001; Muschert, Henry, Bracy, & Peguero, 2013; Muschert & Peguero, 2010; Payne, 2016; Payne, Gottfredson, & Gottfredson, 2003). Thus, the collective relationships between teachers, students, and administrators can create a sense of trust and belonging for a larger community consisting of each of those groups and in turn influence the school's overall effectiveness and efficiency (Gottfredson, 2001; Muschert et al., 2013; Muschert & Peguero, 2010; Payne, 2016; Payne et al., 2003). A school's environment or sense of community is found to be associated with academic interest, self-esteem, academic motivation, delinquency or misbehavior, victimization, conflict resolution, and altruistic behavior at the individual, group, and school levels (Gottfredson, 2001; Muschert et al., 2013; Muschert & Peguero, 2010; Payne, 2016; Payne et al., 2003).

As noted, it is clear that there are disparate experiences associated with school violence and safety threat for the children of immigrants. It is also clear that criminological theoretical approaches do not always foreground inequality. Some criminologists have questioned if a "one-size-fits-all" approach in the utilization of criminology theories is adequate considering the distinct demographic experiences with school violence and safety (Wilcox, Tillyer, & Fisher, 2009; Payne, 2008; Peguero, Popp, & Koo, 2015). Therefore, a growing number of criminologists approach investigating school violence and safety in a manner similar to their community crime, violence, and safety research. The utilization of conventional community criminology theories to investigate school violence and safety, such as 1) social-ecology, 2) social bonds, 3) opportunity, 4) minority threat, and 5) procedural justice have become commonplace; however, the following discussion will specifically highlight the importance of integrating immigration and criminology theories in order to address school violence and ensure safety for all youth.

4.3 Social-Ecology

The social-ecological framework highlights the importance of considering multiple-level factors that surround individual behavior. Bronfenbrenner (1979) hypothesized that in order to understand youth development, the entire social environment in which growth occurs needs to be considered. Bronfenbrenner (1979) argues that a child's development within the context of the system of relationships forms his or her social environment. Under this paradigm, the social environment that a youth interacts with is a primary influence on his or her development. A youth's experience with violence, as well as safety, is not simply directed by individual attitudes and behaviors, but it is also influenced or inhibited by interpersonal relationships, as well as broader social-ecological factors, such as societal, community, institutional, group, and individual (Bronfenbrenner, 1979; Espelage, 2014; Cohen & Espelage, 2020; García Coll et al., 1996; Hong & Eamon, 2012). Ideally, schools are institutions that promote fairness and facilitate educational progress. However, schools are historically characterized by diversity and disparities in students' educational experiences

(Abu El-Haj, 2006, 2015; Kao, Vaquera, & Goyette, 2013; Lee, 2005, 2009; Lee & Zhou, 2015; Lewis & Diamond, 2015; Rios, 2011, 2017; Shedd, 2015; Suárez-Orozco, Suárez-Orozco, & Todorova, 2009).

García Coll and colleagues (1996) argue that researchers must consider the significance of social stratification and inequality when investigating the connections between social environment and youth development. García Coll and colleagues (1996) extend Bronfenbrenner's (1979) social-ecological theoretical approach, asserting that researchers should consider 1) social position (e.g., race, class, and gender), 2) social stratification (e.g., biased treatment), 3) promoting or inhibiting environments (e.g., school), 4) adaptive culture and current demands (e.g., assimilation or acculturation), 5) youth characteristics (e.g., age, psychological characteristics), and 6) family (e.g., structure, functioning) when investigating the role that the social environment has for marginalized youth, such as racial and ethnic minority and immigrant youth. Under this approach, the social environment, including within schools, is particularly important because norms about behavior and climate can influence life-course trajectories, adolescent development, overall well-being, and educational progress (Cohen & Espelage, 2020; Finkelhor, 2014). It also appears that the context of racial and ethnic stratification, inequality, and biased treatment is intrinsic in this aforementioned relationship (Bradshaw, 2013; Filindra, Blanding, & García Coll, 2011; García Coll & Marks, 2012). Thus, the social-ecological environment matters for the children of immigrants' experiences with violence at school.

At the *societal level*, there are harmful processes that have historically marginalized the children of immigrants and contributed to their experiences with violence in school. These societal level factors highlight historical, structural, systemic, and overarching immigration disparities in the United States that are associated with school violence and safety. For instance, heated and controversial social and political debates about U.S. immigration policies may detrimentally influence school relationships and interactions between immigrant families/parents, school friends and classmates, and teachers and administrators (Filindra et al., 2011; Gonzales, 2016; Suárez-Orozco et al., 2009). At the *community level*, because schools are embedded in communities, an unsafe neighborhood environment can also influence school violence and safety. For instance, schools serving predominantly immigrant communities are often embedded in urban communities with higher levels of poverty, unemployment, crime, and violence (Durán, 2013, 2018; Filindra et al., 2011; Gonzales, 2016; Kubrin, Zatz, & Martínez,

2012; Suárez-Orozco et al., 2009). The school's ability and use of economic resources to ensure and enact safety policies are challenged to stem the tide of community violence from entering the school (Durán, 2013, 2018; Muschert & Peguero, 2010; Peguero, 2012b). At the *institutional level*, school climate can influence youth's academic, behavioral, and social outcomes (DiPietro et al., 2015; Durán, 2013, 2018; Hong et al., 2016; Peguero, 2011). The children of immigrants who attend schools where use and sales of illicit substances, violence, and criminal activities are pervasive have limited opportunities for academic success and social mobility, as they are made vulnerable and exposed to that dangerous environment. That environment can also manifest school-related problems, such as fighting and delinquency (DiPietro et al., 2015; Durán, 2013; Hong et al., 2016; Peguero, 2011). The children of immigrants who perceive their schools as fair are less likely to engage in deviant behavior; to the contrary, the children of immigrant youth who experience biased treatment, victimization, and believe that their school sustains disorder are more likely to engage in deviant behavior (Peguero, 2012a, 2013; Peguero & Jiang, 2014; Rios, 2011, 2017). At the *group level*, the children of immigrants who have limited English proficiency may find it difficult to establish friendships with native-born peers and find school group membership (Garver & Noguera, 2015; Kao et al., 2013; Suárez-Orozco et al., 2009). Some suggest that same-ethnicity friendship, shared language, and congruent cultural beliefs could serve as an insulating factor from victimization, with same-ethnicity peers providing social and emotional support (Lee, 2005, 2009; Lee & Zhou, 2015; Garver & Noguera, 2015; Hong et al., 2016; Peguero, 2013); moreover, others suggest that friendships and group involvement with native-born youth could also promote victimization and foster engagement in deviant behavior (DiPietro et al., 2015; Hong et al., 2016; Peguero, 2011). At the *individual level*, the behaviors and student activity, movement, or patterns within the daily school routines may expose the children of immigrants to fear, victimization, and violence (Garver & Noguera, 2015; Hong & Eamon, 2012; Peguero, 2013). For instance, the children of Middle Eastern immigrants encounter religiously biased treatment and ignorance at school, factors that influence their school routines and activities (Abu El-Haj, 2006, 2015; Basford, 2010; Haboush, 2007). Basford (2010) cites an example, describing an incident involving a Middle Eastern immigrant's children who participated in a school book club exchange: they frequently heard students yell, "There go the little terrorists," and observed several people in their math class, including the teacher, laugh loudly at the Muslim American youth who engaged in this mainstream school activity.

4.4 Social Bonds

Hirschi's (1969) social bond theory is based on bridging the link between individuals and conventional social institutions in order to explain delinquent behavior. Social bond theory postulates that individuals are inherently inclined to be deviant (Hirschi, 1969). Thus, the mechanisms that inhibit individuals from yielding to their deviant inclinations warrant particular scrutiny. Hirschi argued that a strong bond to social institutions, such as schools, promotes conformity to conventional norms. Individuals who possess weak or broken social bonds to conventional institutions are more likely to engage in deviant behavior and violence (Hirschi, 1969). According to Hirschi, an individual's bond to social institutions consists of four elements: 1) emotional attachment to parents, peers, and conventional institutions, such as school and work; 2) commitment to long-term educational, occupational, or other conventional goals; 3) involvement in conventional activities, such as work, homework, and hobbies; and 4) belief in the moral validity of the law. While these four elements of social bonds can independently inhibit engagement in deviance, the combined effect of the four elements of the social bond on behavior is greater than the sum of their individual effects. As Hirschi suggests, "The more closely a person is tied to conventional society in any of these ways, the more closely [s/]he is likely to be tied in the other ways" (Hirschi, 1969, p. 27). According to social bond theory, adaptation to mainstream social and cultural expectations, as well as bonding to conventional social institutions, are associated with youth engagement in crime and delinquency; moreover, social bond theory denotes that a strong social bond to social institutions promotes conformity to conventional norms that may be harmful as often as they are beneficial (Hirschi, 1969). Research also demonstrates variations in these four elements of social bonds (i.e., attachment, commitment, involvement, and belief) are found to be associated with school violence and safety for the children of immigrants.

Findings suggest that aspects of school attachment, commitment, involvement, and belief vary by generation. It is argued that immigrants often bring with them a culture of trust for schoolteachers and administration; however, that *attachment* diminishes over generations as immigrant families experience barriers, hurdles, and disparate treatment (Bondy, Peguero, & Johnson, 2019; Kao et al., 2013; Peguero & Bondy, 2011; Portes & Rumbaut, 2014). In general, first-generation youth are more attached to their teachers and schools; however, there is a potential pattern of decreased attachment to teachers and schools among adolescents as their immigrant families assimilate (Bui, 2009, 2015; Bondy et al., 2019; Peguero & Bondy, 2011; Peguero, Bondy, & Shekarkhar, 2017; Watkins & Melde, 2009). Immigrants often instill a strong *commitment* to their children's education because the opportunity for a U.S. education and the subsequent socioeconomic benefits are often primary motivating factors to migrate to the United States (Kao et al., 2013; Peguero et al., 2017; Portes & Rumbaut, 2014). Thus, in general, first-generation youth have stronger commitments to school and their education than their native-born counterparts (Bondy et al., 2019; Kao et al., 2013; Kumi-Yeboah, Brobbey, & Smith, 2020; Peguero et al., 2017; Portes & Rumbaut, 2014; Waters, 2001). It also appears, according to the same studies, that commitment to school is likely to diminish as the children of immigrants assimilate. In general, first-generation adolescents report lower levels of school *involvement* in extracurricular activities; however, there is a pattern of increased school activity as the children of immigrants assimilate (Jiang & Peterson, 2012; Okamoto, Herda, & Hartzog, 2013; Portes & Rumbaut, 2014). In their study, Jiang and Peterson (2012) found that increased school involvement mitigated deviant behavior across immigrant generations, but with two caveats: the type of school activity mattered and the benefits of school activity involvement were strongest for third-plus generation youth. First-generation youth have an increased *belief* that schools are just and fair. First-generation adolescents, in general, have more positive perceptions that the school rules and punishment practices are clear and fair (Peguero et al., 2015; Peguero, 2012a; Peguero & Bondy, 2015). It is argued that immigrants often bring with them a culture of optimism because the motivation for migrating to the United States is one of hope and opportunity, especially in relation to the school system (Crosnoe & Turley, 2011; Kao et al., 2013; Portes & Rumbaut, 2014).

In sum, it appears that the children of immigrants have distinct levels of bonds, often diminishing, to school, which in turn may be having an impact on the relationships between immigration, violence, and safety at school. In a study focusing on the relationship between social control and the school violence immigrant paradox, Peguero and Jiang (2014) find that social control indeed moderated school-based victimization and misconduct across immigrant generations. In essence,

Peguero and Jiang (2014) argue that strengthening school bonds for immigrant youth could result in the amelioration of victimization and misconduct at school.

4.5 Opportunity

Opportunity theory builds on routine activity and lifestyle theoretical frameworks that conceptualize factors associated with victimization. Routine activity theory highlights three necessary factors for crime to occur: 1) the presence and proximity of motivated offenders, 2) the presence of a suitable target, and 3) the absence of a capable guardian (Cho, Hong, Espelage, & Choi, 2017; Peguero, 2009; Popp, 2012a, 2012b; Wilcox et al., 2009). Routine activity theory proposes that victimization stems from the recurrent and prevalent activities that individuals are involved in daily, which increases the likelihood that all three necessary factors will be present. Therefore, it is an individual's routines and activities that increase one's risk of victimization. Similarly, lifestyle theorists suggest that involvement in particular deviant groups or social activities may make a person more susceptible to victimization (Cho et al., 2017; Peguero, 2009; Popp, 2012a, 2012b; Wilcox et al., 2009). Subsequently, researchers have integrated both routine activities and lifestyle theories to better understand the relationship between misbehavior and victimization. The principal logic driving the integration of these two theories in relation to opportunity is centered on four factors that contribute to victimization – 1) suitable targets, 2) exposure, 3) proximity to motivated offenders, and 4) lack of guardianship (Cho et al., 2017; Peguero, 2008, 2009; Popp, 2012a, 2012b; Wilcox et al., 2009). Inequalities associated with socioeconomic and social statuses have been found to moderate these elements of opportunity theory (i.e., target suitability, exposure, proximity to motivated offenders, and guardianship), and these factors are often utilized to understand and address school violence, as well as ensure school safety for students.

There are immigration-generational differences in the relationship between school activities and increased school-based misbehavior. First-generation adolescents are less likely to misbehave while at school but become more likely to misbehave as they assimilate (DiPietro et al., 2015; Peguero, 2013). Jiang and Peterson (2012) explored the role of school involvement with engagement in their community for the children of immigrants. They suggest that increased school involvement mitigates deviant behavior across immigrant generations, but with two caveats: the type of school activity mattered and the benefits of school involvement were strongest for third-plus generation youth. Peguero (2013) found that target suitability is linked to school-based adolescent victimization across immigrant generations, those relationships are dependent on the type of school activity. As noted in the prior section with social control, the level and type of engagement in school-based activities vary across generations. First-generation immigrants are less likely to engage in extracurricular activities (Jiang & Peterson, 2012; Okamoto et al., 2013; Portes & Rumbaut, 2014).

Peguero (2013) suggests that generational status also matters in the type of school activity adolescents choose. The relevance of language, cultural, and social understandings necessary to engage in academic, sport, and club school activities vary. The study reveals the complexed notion that more involvement in academics (e.g., school band, newspaper), sports, and club activities at school could increase the vulnerability of the children of immigrants to victimization at school. This finding could easily be interpreted as contradictory to prior social control and school-based victimization and misconduct research; however, there are important nuances that need to be highlighted. As will be discussed in the next section, there is the potential role of the *threat* of minorities, and particularly immigrants, that may be associated with school violence and safety research. Thus, it is possible that native-born students may perceive school-based extracurricular activities as a valuable educational opportunity that the children of immigrants are threatening to take away from native-born students.

4.6 Minority Threat

Minority threat is a prominent hypothesis that may explain interracial conflict or violence and the overrepresentation of minorities within the justice system (Feldmeyer & Ulmer, 2011; Jacobs, Malone, & Iles, 2012; Leiber, Peck, & Rodriguez, 2016; Petersen & Ward, 2015; Wang & Mears, 2010). Minority threat theorists suggest that a growing minority population (e.g., racial and ethnic or immigrant) poses a threat to the majority group; in this case, White Americans, who, perceiving a growing threat, may take action to reduce it (Blalock, 1967; Liska, 1992; Tolnay & Beck, 1995). Blalock (1967) discussed that the source of perceived minority threat can take on two different forms: economic threat and political threat. Blalock (1967) hypothesized that as a result of competition for opportunities, jobs, and other economic resources, White Americans increasingly feel that their economic dominance is threatened. Second, Blalock (1967) indicates that as minorities gain political power, White Americans have a reciprocal belief that their political hegemony is being threatened. For interracial conflict or violence, researchers have argued that racial riots, lynchings, hate crimes, and interpersonal violence have been partially explained by an increasing number of competitive minorities seeking employment and economic opportunities (Feldmeyer & Ulmer, 2011; Jacobs et al., 2012; Leiber et al., 2016; Petersen & Ward, 2015; Wang & Mears, 2010). For increased social control via the justice system, stringent justice policies, such as allocation of police resources and funding, police presence, arrests, convictions, and severe prison sentences, have become mechanisms to control a growing minority population (Feldmeyer & Ulmer, 2011; Jacobs et al., 2012; Leiber et al., 2016; Petersen & Ward, 2015; Wang & Mears, 2010). Some have argued that the minority threat hypothesis is also evident within the U.S. school system.

As the minority population increases within a school, so do parents' decisions to move residences or to move their children to another school. Further, historical battles over bussing ensue, as well as punitive school discipline (Olzak, Shanahan, & West, 1994; Renzulli & Evans, 2005; Payne & Welch, 2010; Welch, 2018). There is also a history and persistent trend of minority inequality, segregation, interracial conflict, and separatism in the U.S. schools (Buchmann, Condron, & Roscigno, 2010; Kao et al., 2013; Lewis & Diamond, 2015). It also appears that minorities often attend schools that are like "prisons" because these schools sustain increased police presence, security measures, surveillance, and stringent punishment policies (Noguera, 2009; Portillos, González, & Peguero, 2012; Rios, 2011, 2017). Payne and Welch (2010) find that school disciplinary actions tended to be much more punitive in schools with greater levels of minority students. Moreover, they report that schools with a greater proportion of racial and ethnic minorities are less likely to use restorative practices in discipline; more likely to focus on severe punishment; more likely to use zero-tolerance policies; more likely to use extreme measures of action, such as calling the police for minor offenses; and less likely to refer students with behavioral issues to a school counselor (Payne & Welch, 2010; Welch, 2018).

The "immigrant threat" paradigm is also evident in the justice and school systems. Kubrin et al. (2012) argue that there has been a significant increase in creating, implementing, and enforcing stringent criminal justice policies that are controlling immigrants and their children. Some suggest that the growing population of immigrants, especially in a "post-9/11 society," has been the catalyst for a social, political, economic, and criminal justice "war" on immigration and immigrants (Chavez, 2013; Kubrin et al., 2012; Stacey, Carbone-Lopez, & Rosenfeld, 2011). At the federal level, there are unprecedented enforcement policies that currently target immigrants and their children with increased employment raids, detentions, and deportations, as well as imposing a public discourse establishing a surge of "illegal immigrants" (Chaudry et al., 2010; Chavez, 2013; Kubrin et al., 2012; Stacey et al., 2011). At the state level, Florida, Texas, California, Alabama, and Arizona create, implement, and enforce policies that deny basic health and social services to immigrants and their children (Chaudry et al., 2010; Chavez, 2013; Chavez & Provine, 2009; Stacey et al., 2011). It also appears that policies that address the threat against immigration and immigrant families are also extending into the school system. Filindra and colleagues (2011) argue that the effects of political ideology and policies that marginalize immigrants have detrimental consequences for their children's overall well-being, school experiences, and educational progress. It appears that as populations of immigrants increase within some schools, the children of immigrants report increased harassment, bullying, and aggression from native-born and White American student peers, as well as detrimental treatment from school faculty and administrators (Abu El-Haj, 2006, 2015; Basford, 2010; Filindra et al., 2011; Lee, 2005, 2009; Olsen, 2008; Portes & Rumbaut, 2014; Rong & Preissle, 2008; Suárez-Orozco et al., 2009). Research also suggests that, even after controlling for student misbehavior, the children of immigrants have increased odds of being disciplined at school (Peguero & Shekarkhar, 2011; Peguero et al., 2015). As will be discussed in the next section, the disproportionate punishment of the children of immigrants may also be reflective of *procedural justice* within schools.

4.7 Procedural Justice

Procedural justice theory hypothesizes that individuals who perceive authority figures in procedurally fair and just manners are more likely to view authority figures as legitimate (Tyler, 1990, 2009, 2011). Belief, perception, and evaluation of legitimacy are important because they are related to the public's trust, satisfaction, support, and compliance with regard to authority figures (Tyler, 1990, 2009, 2011). Procedural justice is conceptually composed of two board concepts: 1) quality of decision making and 2) quality of interpersonal treatment (Tyler, 1990, 2009, 2011); moreover, there are four principles or "pillars" for procedural justice: 1) being fair in processes, 2) being transparent in actions, 3) providing opportunities for voice, and 4) being impartial in decision making. Quality of decision making within a procedural justice theoretical framework consists of individuals perceiving and believing that they are being treated fairly and justly when authority figures exercise their authority in neutral and unbiased manners (Tyler, 1990, 2009, 2011). Tyler (1990) argues, "People are seeking a level playing field in which no one is unfairly advantaged" (p. 94). Quality of interpersonal treatment within a procedural justice theoretical framework consists of the degree to which individuals perceive and believe that they are treated with respect and dignity by authority figures (Tyler, 1990, 2009, 2011). Procedures are perceived as fair and just when people feel as though they are treated respectfully and are allowed to participate in the decision-making process because they can ascribe status recognition to those as authority figures. The concept of procedural justice has been researched and applied to an array of social institutions, such as law enforcement, courts, corrections, and legislation; however, there has been an increasing use of procedural justice by authority figures within schools.

When applied to students and schools, procedural justice generally refers to student beliefs about the fairness of school rules and application of discipline practices (see, e.g., Kupchik, 2010, 2016; Muschert & Peguero, 2010; Peguero, 2012a; Peguero & Bracy, 2015; Portillos et al., 2012; Rios, 2011, 2017). Youth who perceive school rules and discipline practices as just and fair have improved interpersonal relationships with teachers and administrators, strong bonds to their school and education, increased perceptions of school safety and educational achievement, and decreased school misbehavior (Hong & Eamon, 2012; Payne, 2008, 2016; Payne et al., 2003). Conversely, students who perceive the school rules and discipline practices as unjust or unfair have poorer educational progress, engage in student misbehavior, and are more vulnerable to being victimized at school (Kupchik, 2010, 2016; Payne, 2008, 2016; Payne et al., 2003; Peguero & Bracy, 2015; Popp, 2012a; Portillos et al., 2012; Rios, 2011, 2017).

Prior research demonstrates that the children of immigrants have distinct perceptions of school procedural justice. Research demonstrates that immigrant youth, in general, have more positive perceptions that their school procedural justice practices are clear and fair (Peguero, 2012a; Peguero & Bondy, 2015; Suárez-Orozco et al., 2009); however, those positive perceptions about school procedural justice practices diminish as the children of immigrants, especially Black/African American and Latina/o American youth, continue in school (Peguero, 2012a; Peguero & Bondy, 2015). Some have argued that the "Americanization" process informs the children of immigrants' experiences as they witness biased punishment practices by school faculty and administrators (Peguero, 2012a; Peguero & Bondy, 2015; Suárez-Orozco et al., 2009). Moreover, in some schools, the children of immigrants come to distrust school faculty, administrators, and security personnel (Portillos et al., 2012; Suárez-Orozco et al., 2009). Some children of immigrants report that school faculty, administrators, and security personnel can wield threats of deportation against them or family members as a form of surveillance and control, a practice that can instill fear and distrust in the children of immigrants (Gonzales, 2016; Gonzales et al., 2013). As a consequence, school procedural justice practices can have real implications for the children of immigrants' ability to trust school faculty, administrators, and security personnel who are there to address violence and ensure their safety while at school.

In this chapter about utilizing criminology theories when understanding and addressing the relationships between immigration and school safety, we explicated the importance of criminology theories (i.e., social-ecology, social bonds, opportunity, minority threat, and procedural justice) for understanding and ensuring the children of immigrants' safety and well-being while at school. Both past and contemporary research examine the ongoing uneasiness of immigrant populations and their influence on the U.S. public school system (Apple & Franklin, 2004; Kao et al., 2013; Peguero & Bondy, 2015). Additionally, the "one-size-fits-all" or "standardized" approach toward making schools safe may not be effective considering the distinct vulnerabilities that the children of immigrants face in the U.S. school system (Peguero, 2013; Peguero & Jiang, 2014). It is important for researchers not only to utilize criminology theories to understand the causes and correlates of school safety but also to keep in mind that the children of immigrants face unique challenges and complex realities or experiences with school violence and safety. Of course, utilizing criminology theories to pursue safety is paramount for all youth; however, it is vital to also ensure the safety of marginalized and vulnerable youth. Considering that it is projected that within the youth population, one in three youth will have at least one immigrant parent, understanding the causes contributing to victimization and the factors that ensure safety for the fastest-growing marginalized segments of the U.S. youth population is imperative.

References

Abu El-Haj, T. R. (2006). Race, politics, and Arab American youth: Shifting frameworks for conceptualizing educational equity. *Educational Policy, 20,* 13–34.

Abu El-Haj, T. R. (2015). *Unsettled belonging: Educating Palestinian American youth after 9/11.* Chicago, IL: University of Chicago Press.

Apple, M., & Franklin, B. (2004). Curricular history and social control. In M. Apple (Ed.), *Ideology and curriculum* (pp. 59–76). New York: Routledge Falmer.

Basford, L. (2010). From mainstream to east African charter: Cultural and religious experiences of Somali youth in U.S. schools. *Journal of School Choice, 4,* 485–509.

Blalock, H. M. (1967). *Toward a theory of minority group relations.* New York: Wiley.

Bondy, J. M., Peguero, A. A., & Johnson, B. E. (2019). The children of immigrants' bonding to school: Examining the roles of assimilation, gender, race, ethnicity, and social bonds. *Urban Education, 54,* 592–622.

Bradshaw, C. P. (2013). Preventing bullying through positive behavioral interventions and supports (PBIS): A multi-tiered approach to prevention and integration. *Theory into Practice, 52,* 288–295.

Bronfenbrenner, U. (1979). *The ecology of human development: Experiments by nature and design.* Cambridge, MA: Harvard University Press.

Buchmann, C., Condron, D., & Roscigno, V. (2010). Shadow education, American style: Test preparation, the SAT and college enrollment. *Social Forces, 89,* 435–462.

Bui, H. N. (2009). Parent-child conflicts, school troubles, and delinquency among immigrants. *Crime and Delinquency, 55,* 412–441.

Bui, H. N. (2015). Economic opportunities and immigrant youth violence. *Youth Violence and Juvenile Justice, 13*(4), 391–408.

Chaudry, A, Capps, R., Pedroza, J. M., Castañeda, R. M., Santos, R., & Scott, M. M. (2010). *Facing our future children in the aftermath of immigration enforcement.* Washington, DC: The Urban Institute.

Chavez, L. (2013). *The Latino threat: Constructing immigrants, citizens and the nation.* Stanford, CA: Stanford University Press.

Chavez, J. M., & Provine, D. M. (2009). Race and the response of state legislatures to unauthorized immigrants. *The Annals of the American Academy of Political and Social Science, 623,* 78–92.

Cho, S., Hong, J. S., Espelage, D. L., & Choi, K. S. (2017). Applying the lifestyle routine activities theory to understand physical and nonphysical peer victimization. *Journal of Aggression, Maltreatment & Trauma, 26*(3), 297–315.

Cohen, J., & Espelage, D. L. (2020). *Feeling safe in school: Bullying and violence prevention around the world.* Cambridge, MA: Harvard Education Press.

Crosnoe, R., & Turley, R. N. L. (2011). K – 12 educational outcomes of immigrant youth. *The Future of Children, 21*(1), 129.

Desmond, S., & Kubrin, C. E. (2009). The power of place: Immigrant communities and adolescent violence. *Sociological Quarterly, 50,* 581–607.

DiPietro, S., & McGloin, J. M. (2012). Differential susceptibility? Immigrant youth and peer influence. *Criminology, 50,* 711–742.

DiPietro, S., Slocum, L. A., & Esbensen, F. (2015). School context and violence: Does immigrant status matter? *Youth Violence and Juvenile Justice, 13,* 299–322.

Durán, R. J. (2013). *Gang life in two cities: An insider's journey.* New York: Columbia University Press.

Durán, R. J. (2018). *The gang paradox: Inequalities and miracles on the U.S.-Mexico border.* New York: Columbia University Press.

Espelage, D. L. (2014). Ecological theory: Preventing youth bullying, aggression, & victimization. *Theory into Practice, 53,* 257–264.

Feldmeyer, B., & Ulmer, J. T. (2011). Racial/ethnic threat and federal sentencing. *Journal of Research in Crime and Delinquency, 48,* 238–270.

Filindra, A., Blanding, D., & García Coll, C. (2011). The power of context: State-level policies and politics and the educational performance of the children of immigrants in the United States. *Harvard Educational Review, 81,* 407–437.

Finkelhor, D. (2014). *Childhood victimization: Violence, crime and abuse in the lives of young people.* New York: Oxford University Press.

García Coll, C., Lamberty, G., Jenkins, R., McAdoo, H. P., Crnic, K., Wasik, B. H., & García, H. V. (1996). An integrative model for the study of developmental competencies in minority children. *Child Development, 67,* 1891–1914.

García Coll, C., & Marks, A. K. (2012). *The immigrant paradox in children and adolescents: Is becoming American a developmental risk?* Washington, DC: American Psychological Association Press.

Garver, R., & Noguera, P. (2015). Supported and unsafe: The impact of educational structures for immigrant students on school safety. *Youth Violence and Juvenile Justice, 13*(4), 323–344.

Gonzales, R. G. (2016). *Lives in limbo: Undocumented and coming of age in America.* Berkeley, CA: University of California Press.

Gonzales, R. G., Suárez-Orozco, C., & Dedios-Sanguineti, M. C. (2013). Contextualizing concepts of mental health among undocumented immigrant youth in the United States. *American Behavioral Scientist, 57,* 1173–1198.

Gottfredson, D. C. (2001). *Schools and delinquency.* New York: Cambridge University Press.

Haboush, K. L. (2007). Working with Arab American families: Culturally competent practice for school psychologists. *Psychology in the Schools, 44,* 183–198.

Hirschi, T. (1969). *Causes of delinquency.* Berkeley, CA: University of California Press.

Hong, J. S., & Eamon, M. K. (2012). Students' perceptions of unsafe schools: An ecological systems analysis. *Journal of Child and Family Studies, 21*(3), 428–438.

Hong, J. S., Merrin, G. J., Peguero, A. A., Gonzalez-Prendes, A. A., & Lee, N. Y. (2016). Exploring the social-ecological determinants of physical fighting in U.S. schools: What about youth in immigrant families? *Child & Youth Care Forum, 45*(2), 279–299.

Hong, J. S., Peguero, A. A., Choi, S., Lanesskog, D., Espelage, D., & Lee, N. Y. (2014). School bullying and peer victimization of Latino and Asian American youth: A social-ecological framework. *Journal of School Violence, 13*, 315–338.

Jacobs, D., Malone, C., & Iles, G. (2012). Race and imprisonment: Vigilante violence, minority threat, and racial politics. *The Sociological Quarterly, 53*, 166–187.

Jiang, X., & Peterson, R. (2012). Beyond participation: The association between school extracurricular activities and involvement in violence across generations of immigration. *Journal of Youth and Adolescence, 41*, 362–378.

Kao, G., Vaquera, E., & Goyette, K. (2013). *Education and immigration*. Malden, MA: Policy Press.

Kubrin, C. E., & Desmond, S. A. (2015). The power of place revisited: Why immigrant communities have lower levels of adolescent violence. *Youth Violence and Juvenile Justice, 13*, 345–366.

Kubrin, C., Zatz, M., & Martínez, R. (2012). *Punishing immigrants: Policy, politics, and injustice*. New York: New York University Press.

Kumi-Yeboah, A., Brobbey, G., & Smith, P. (2020). Exploring factors that facilitate acculturation strategies and academic success of West African immigrant youth in urban schools. *Education and Urban Society, 52*(1), 21–50.

Kupchik, A. (2010). *Homeroom security: School discipline in an age of fear*. New York: New York University Press.

Kupchik, A. (2016). *The real school safety problem: The long-term consequences of harsh school punishment*. Oakland: University of California Press.

Lee, S. J. (2005). *Up against Whiteness: Race, school and immigrant youth*. New York: Teachers College Press.

Lee, S. J. (2009). *Unraveling the model minority stereotype: Listening to Asian American youth*. New York: Teachers College Press.

Lee, S. J., & Zhou, M. (2015). *The Asian American achievement paradox*. New York: Russell Sage Foundation.

Leiber, M. J., Peck, J. H., & Rodriguez, N. (2016). Minority threat and juvenile court outcomes. *Crime & Delinquency, 62*(1), 54–80.

Lewis, A. E., & Diamond, J. B. (2015). *Despite the best intentions: How racial inequality thrives in good schools*. Oxford: Oxford University Press.

Liska, A. E. (1992). *Social threat and social control*. Albany: SUNY Press.

Miller, H. V., & Peguero, A. A. (2018). *Routledge handbook on immigration and crime*. New York: Routledge Falmer.

Muschert, G. W., Henry, S., Bracy, N. L., & Peguero, A. A. (2013). *Responses to school violence: Confronting the Columbine effect*. Boulder, CO: Lynne Reinner Publishers.

Muschert, G. W., & Peguero, A. A. (2010). The Columbine effect and school anti-violence policy. *Research in Social Problems & Public Policy, 17*, 117–148.

Noguera, P. A. (2009). *The trouble with Black boys: And other reflections on race, equity, and the future of public education.* San Francisco, CA: Jossey-Bass.

Okamoto, D. G., Herda, D., & Hartzog, C. (2013). Beyond good grades: School composition and immigrant youth participation in extracurricular activities. *Social Science Research, 42,* 155–168.

Olsen, L. (2008). *Made in America: Immigrant students in our public schools.* New York: New York University Press.

Olzak, S., Shanahan, S., & West, E. (1994). School-desegregation, interracial exposure, and antibusing activity in contemporary urban America. *American Journal of Sociology, 100,* 196–241.

Payne, A. A. (2008). A multilevel model of the relationships among communal school disorder, student bonding, and delinquency. *Journal of Research in Crime and Delinquency, 45,* 429–455.

Payne, A. A. (2016). *Creating and sustaining a positive and communal school climate: Contemporary research, present obstacles, and future directions.* Retrieved from www.ncjrs.gov/pdffiles1/nij/250209.pdf

Payne, A. A., Gottfredson, D. C., & Gottfredson, G. D. (2003). Schools as communities: The relationships among communal school disorder, student bonding, and school disorder. *Criminology, 41,* 749–778.

Payne, A. A., & Welch, K. (2010). Modeling the effects of racial threat on punitive and restorative school discipline practices. *Criminology, 48,* 1019–1062.

Peguero, A. A. (2008). Is immigrant status relevant in school violence research? An analysis with Latino students. *Journal of School Health, 78,* 397–404.

Peguero, A. A. (2009). Victimizing the children of immigrants: Latino and Asian American student victimization. *Youth & Society, 41,* 186–208.

Peguero, A. A. (2011). Immigration, schools, and violence: Assimilation and student misbehavior. *Sociological Spectrum, 31,* 695–717.

Peguero, A. A. (2012a). The children of immigrants' diminishing perceptions of just and fair punishment. *Punishment & Society, 14,* 429–451.

Peguero, A. A. (2012b). Schools, bullying, and inequality: Intersecting factors and complexities with the stratification of youth victimization at school. *Sociology Compass, 6,* 402–412.

Peguero, A. A. (2013). An adolescent victimization immigrant paradox?: School-based routines, lifestyles, and victimization across immigration generations. *Journal of Youth and Adolescence, 42,* 1759–1773.

Peguero, A. A., & Bondy, J. M. (2011). Immigration and students' relationship with teachers. *Education and Urban Society, 43,* 165–183.

Peguero, A. A., & Bondy, J. M. (2015). Schools, justice, and immigrant students: Assimilation, race, ethnicity, gender, and perceptions of fairness and order. *Teachers College Record, 117,* 1–42.

Peguero, A. A., Bondy, J. M., & Shekarkhar, Z. (2017). Punishing Latina/o youth: School justice, fairness, order, dropping out, and gender disparities. *Hispanic Journal of Behavioral Sciences, 39*(1), 98–125.

Peguero, A. A., & Bracy, N. L. (2015). School order, justice, and education: Climate, discipline practices, and dropping out. *Journal of Research on Adolescence, 25*(3), 412–426.

Peguero, A. A., & Hong, J. S. (2019). Are violence and disorder at school placing adolescents within immigrant families at higher risk of dropping out? *Journal of School Violence, 18*(2), 241–258.

Peguero, A. A., & Jiang, X. (2014). Social control across immigrant generations: Adolescent violence at school and examining the immigrant paradox. *Journal of Criminal Justice, 42*(3), 276–287.

Peguero, A. A., & Shekarkhar, Z. (2011). Latino/a student misbehavior and school punishment. *Hispanic Journal of Behavioral Sciences, 33*(1), 54–70.

Peguero, A. A., Shekarkhar, Z., Popp, A. M., & Koo, D. J. (2015). Punishing the children of immigrants: Race, ethnicity, generational status, and student misbehavior and school discipline. *Journal of Immigrant & Refugee Studies: Special Issue, Immigration and Civil Society, 13*(2), 200–220.

Petersen, N., & Ward, R. (2015). The transmission of historical racial violence: Lynching, civil rights – era terror, and contemporary interracial homicide. *Race & Justice, 5*, 114–143.

Popp, A. M. (2012a). The difficulty in measuring suitable targets when modeling victimization. *Violence and Victims, 27*(5), 689–709.

Popp, A. M. (2012b). The effects of exposure, proximity, and capable guardians on the risk of bullying victimization. *Youth Violence and Juvenile Justice, 10*(4), 315–332.

Portes, A., & Rumbaut, R. (2014). *Immigrant America: A portrait.* Berkeley, CA: University of California Press.

Portillos, E., González, J. C., & Peguero, A. A. (2012). Crime control strategies in school: Chicanos/as perceptions and criminalization. *The Urban Review, 44*(2), 171–188.

Rengifo, A. F., & Fratello, J. (2015). Perceptions of the police by immigrant youth: Looking at stop-and-frisk and beyond using a New York city sample. *Youth Violence and Juvenile Justice, 13*(4), 409–427.

Renzulli, L., & Evans, L. (2005). School choice, charter schools, and white flight. *Social Problems, 52*(3), 398–418.

Rios, V. M. (2011). *Punished: Policing the lives of Black and Latino boys.* New York: New York University Press.

Rios, V. M. (2017). *Human targets: Schools, police, and the criminalization of Latino youth.* Chicago, IL: The University of Chicago Press.

Rong, X., & Preissle, J. (2008). *Educating immigrant students in the 21st century: What we need to know to meet the challenges.* Thousand Oaks, CA: Corwin Press.

Sampson, R. J. (2008). Rethinking crime and immigration. *Contexts, 7*, 28–33.

Shedd, C. (2015). *Unequal city: Race, schools, and perceptions of injustice.* New York: Russell Sage Foundation.

Stacey, M., Carbone-Lopez, K., & Rosenfeld, R. (2011). Demographic change and ethnically motivated crime: The impact of immigration on anti-Hispanic hate crime in the United States. *Journal of Contemporary Criminal Justice, 27*, 278–298.

Suárez-Orozco, C., Suárez-Orozco, M., & Todorova, I. (2009). *Learning a new land: Immigrant students in American society.* Cambridge, MA: Harvard University Press.

Tolnay, S. E., & Beck, E. M. (1995). *A festival of violence: An analysis of southern lynchings, 1882–1930*. Urbana, IL: University of Illinois Press.

Tyler, T. R. (1990). *Why people obey the law: Procedural justice, legitimacy, and compliance*. New Haven: Yale University Press.

Tyler, T. R. (2009). Ethnicity and perspectives on legal authority. In S. Demoulin, J. P. Leyens, & J. F. Dovidio (Eds.), *Intergroup misunderstandings: Impact of divergent social realities*. Philadelphia: Psychology Press.

Tyler, T. R. (2011). *Why people cooperate*. Princeton, NJ: Princeton University Press.

Wang, X., & Mears, D. P. (2010). Examining the direct and interactive effects of changes in racial and ethnic threat on sentencing decisions. *Journal of Research in Crime and Delinquency, 47*(4), 522–557.

Waters, M. (2001). *Black identities: West Indian immigrant dreams and American realities*. Boston, MA: Harvard University Press.

Watkins, A. M., & Melde, C. (2009). Immigrants, assimilation, and perceived school disorder: An examination of the "other" ethnicities. *Journal of Criminal Justice, 37*(6), 627–635.

Welch, K. (2018). The effect of minority threat on risk management and the "new disciplinology" in schools. *Journal of Criminal Justice, 59*, 12–17.

Wilcox, P., Tillyer, M. S., & Fisher, B. S. (2009). Gendered opportunity? Adolescent school-based victimization. *Journal of Research in Crime and Delinquency, 46*, 245–269.

Wright, K. A., & Rodriguez, N. (2014). A closer look at the paradox: Examining immigration and youth reoffending in Arizona. *Justice Quarterly, 31*(5), 882–904.

Zhou, M. (1997). Growing up American: The challenge confronting immigrant children and children of immigrants. *Annual Review of Sociology, 23*, 63–95.

Chapter 5

The Implications and Importance of Considering Immigration With School Safety

In this chapter, we discuss the implications and importance of considering immigration as schools move forward to ameliorate violence and pursue safety for the children of immigrants. First, we discuss the implications for faculty, staff, administrators, and policymakers. Second, we highlight how to specifically think about the connection between immigration and prominent school safety programs or approaches. Third, we make an argument that any policy efforts that seek to provide safe and healthy schools for all youth, including the children of immigrants, must consider educational success, progress, and well-being as key components of school safety.

5.1 Educational Faculty, Staff, Administrators, and Policymakers

Throughout this discussion, we have highlighted the U.S. sociopolitical landscape that contextualizes the lives of immigrants and their children. We have highlighted that the children of immigrants are vulnerable to violence and marginalization. Young (2011) advocated that because differential privilege is perpetuated by the process of schooling, teachers and administrators committed to educational equality and providing healthy, safe learning environments must "take responsibility." This means that school personnel should consider the role of immigration in association with their own behaviors and actions, address stereotypical immigrant images and myths, equalize policy enforcement, and work to change attitudes and practices (p. 151). Educational equity for the children of immigrants and breaking the cycle of marginalization must be actively pursued by schools in the form of inclusion, empathy, understanding, and protection with their learning, as well as socialization.

Research on the children of immigrants suggests that they often learn from teachers and peers that they are "outsiders" to the nation – even if born in the United States (Gonzales, 2016; Olsen, 2008; Suárez-Orozco, Suárez-Orozco, & Todorova, 2009). Conducted in both traditional and new destination sites, these studies find that the children of immigrants' school relationships are shaped by broader political discourses and practices on immigration. For example, the children of immigrants and their parents are often taunted by school staff, teachers, and students who use racial slurs and make comments such as "go back to your own country" (Gonzales, 2016; Olsen, 2008; Suárez-Orozco et al., 2009). It is also evident that some teachers and administrators punish, discipline, or publicly humiliate the children of immigrants when they speak their native language (Gonzales, 2016; Peguero, Shekarkhar, Popp, & Koo, 2015; Olsen, 2008; Suárez-Orozco et al., 2009). It is in this type of a school climate that the American Psychological Association (APA, 2012) reports xenophobia as an increasing and serious problem for the children of immigrants in U.S. schools, which has detrimental effects on learning and safety. Teachers and administrators who are concerned with addressing the harassment directed at the children of immigrants should not only respond to such forms of violence and harassment; they must also be proactive by establishing and sustaining a school climate of inclusion and tolerance.

In multicultural societies, schools play a powerful role in promoting broader societal discourses that define the necessary qualities and limits of citizenship and social belonging. This suggests that faculty, staff, administrators, and educational policymakers focused on reducing violence against the children of immigrants, as well as ensuring their safety, should recognize the transactions between the macro political context and micro lived experiences of the children of immigrants in order to create new dispositions and identities, as well as more inclusive notions of citizenship and belonging (Zembylas, 2010, 2012). Without an examination of the relationship between emotions, shifting demographics, and negative embodied practices directed at the children of immigrants, possibilities for faculty, staff, administrators, and educational policymakers who create healthy climates, equitable schools, and safe classrooms will be lost. Moreover, faculty, staff, administrators, and educational policymakers who continue to separate emotion from pedagogical practices and multicultural competencies are inadequate to address change within an increasingly diverse world (Zembylas, 2010, 2012). If educators and policymakers wish to

prepare faculty, staff, and administrators to challenge and change existing societal inequities for the children of immigrants, the preparation
of school personnel must include opportunities for individual and collective self-reflection and the examination of the blurring of emotions
and harassment.

Instead of treating harassment against the children of immigrants as
one-off incidents that can adequately be addressed through disciplinary
sanctions, faculty, staff, administrators, and educational policymakers
should prepare students to identify how the broader socio-political
context around immigration can be embodied in the day-to-day interactions of school life and to explore the possibilities that are opened
up for interrupting practices that exclude others. Boler and Zembylas
(2003) proposed that a curriculum of *discomfort* engages students to
analyze the emotional dimensions that frame and shape habits and routines complicit with the marginalization and vulnerabilities endured
by the children of immigrants. Preventing violence and harassment,
as well as ensuring the safety of the children of immigrants while in
school, requires educating faculty and administrators to interrogate the
feelings that maintain particular forms of relationality between "us"
and "them," as well as "American" or "citizen" and immigrant. Educational strategies must be augmented by a consideration of teaching,
administrating, counseling, and working with students and families in
a manner "informed by emotion that resists unjust systems and practices as well as emotion that helps create a more fair and just world in
our classrooms and everyday lives" (Zembylas, 2012, p. 174). Moreover, for harmful actions that maintain boundaries between "us and
them" and "citizen and immigrant," educational policymakers should
help teachers and administrators recognize the ways that xenophobia
structures their own experiences, along with those of the children of
immigrants. Stevens and Stovall (2011) proposed that learning about
citizenship as a phenomenon occurring in a complex interplay of
interests and power would benefit all students. They argued that the
formation of citizenship identities is socially embedded within learning processes that could facilitate potential teacher and administrator candidates to socialize and educate all students to dismiss or be
critical of anti-immigrant discourses and enhance inclusive interactions and criteria for belonging. For example, prospective teachers
and administrators can be asked to consider signs reading, "Welcome
to America . . . now speak English!" and to respond to questions
that include why the sign is there, what is it trying to communicate,
and what the surrounding global and local contexts of immigration,

language, and citizenship embedded in the sign are (Stevens & Stovall, 2011, p. 295). When such signs are read alongside instances of backlash against immigrants and their children, teachers and administrators could encourage students to question the larger environment, examine the constant dynamic between discourses and practices of exclusion, and produce alternative realities. Thus, educational policymakers who seek to address the violence and harassment against the children of immigrants in schools should develop a curriculum that trains teachers' and administrators' understanding of larger patterns of xenophobia and exclusion by fostering democracy and inclusion.

5.2 Zero-Tolerance and Control Approaches

Foucault (1977) is often referred to as conceptualizing this sociological shift toward a "disciplinary society" where he is cited as stating, "Factories, schools, barracks, hospitals, which all resemble prisons" (p. 228). Moreover, Simon (2010) argues, "The technologies, discourses, and metaphors of crime and criminal justice have become more visible features of all kinds of institutions" (p. 4). These social institutions, including schools, have incorporated policies, mechanisms, techniques, and an overall culture of social control (Kupchik, 2010, 2016; Morris, 2016; Rios, 2011, 2017; Shedd, 2015). The influence of government approaches to crime and violence in nationwide policies, such as zero-tolerance, along with financial incentives to schools for police and other security measures (such as those provided in the "Secure Our Schools" Act of 2000) has become a pervasive response to the public concern and fear of youth violence within schools. As noted, Simon (2010) illustrates how governing through violence has influenced rules and practices in schools across social strata; he states that "the very real violence of a few schools concentrated in zones of hardened poverty and social disadvantage has provided a 'truth' of school crime that circulates across whole school systems" (p. 210). However, the expanding use of zero-tolerance and social control within schools raises concern because of unintended consequences for youth who attend highly controlled and securitized schools. Research also indicates that surveillance and security, such as police, cameras, and metal detectors, create a "prison-like" institutional atmosphere or environment, especially for schools located in disadvantaged or urban areas (Morris, 2016; Noguera, 2009; Portillos, González, & Peguero, 2012; Rios, 2011, 2017; Shedd, 2015).

Although social control practices, highly securitized schools, and zero-tolerance are school safety policies ostensibly intended to protect students and ensure a safe learning environment, many argue that these social control policies have disproportionately impacted racial and ethnic minority youth, as well as the children of immigrants (Crenshaw, Ocen, & Nanda, 2015; Gregory, Skiba, & Noguera, 2010; Kim et al., 2010; Peguero & Hong, 2019; Peguero et al., 2015; Portillos et al., 2012; Rios, 2011, 2017; Shedd, 2015; Skiba, Horner, Chung, & Rausch, 2011). Disproportionate punishment (e.g., referral, suspension, expulsion) could steer students toward social exclusion, educational failure, and life-long economic hardship (Crenshaw et al., 2015; Gregory et al., 2010; Morris, 2016; Noguera, 2009; Rios, 2011, 2017; Shedd, 2015; Skiba et al., 2011). Considering that it is estimated that currently one in four students have at least one immigrant parent (U.S. Census, 2017), addressing this educational and justice inequality of disproportionate punishment for the children of immigrants is essential. Of course, we do not discount the argued importance of disciplining adolescents who engage in deviant, delinquent, or violent behavior. However, Muschert and Peguero (2010) also argue, "The difficulty in understanding the catalysts for school antiviolence policy development is that the line between caring and undue control is unclear" (p. 123).

There are four recommendations associated with immigration that should be considered by those schools that incorporate zero-tolerance and stringent social control policies. First, administrators should recognize the possibility of criminalization in their efforts to secure school safety. It is not unreasonable to believe that the children of immigrants are assimilating or learning lessons of inequality. Kupchik (2010) stressed that racial and ethnic minority youth in U.S. schools may be learning the "wrong" lesson when it comes to school discipline practices by suggesting that "this lesson encourages passivity and uncritical acceptance of authority, which bodes poorly for the future of democratic participation" (p. 7). Thus, faculty, staff, administrators, and security personnel should consider that the children of immigrants are particularly vulnerable to the impact of expulsion and exclusion as they administer sanctions. Second, schools should function and look like educational institutions rather than quasi-prisons. Students recognize larger structural inequalities evident in society, and securitizing schools with metal bars, metal detectors, cameras, and school resource officers creates a disjunction and can alienate students. Worse than alienation, school securitization can lead some students to internalize their role in society as future criminals, for they learn that schools (like society) do not trust them to be responsible citizens. It should be noted here that when teachers are not focusing on personal safety, they can focus on educating students. This is particularly relevant when the children of immigrants are in heightened fear of deportation, while other students, faculty, staff, and security personnel use threats of deportation as a means of harassment or control. Third, since security measures can have positive impacts on safety, we can acknowledge that cameras and surveillance techniques can be helpful as a means of monitoring; however, we would do well to train security guards and school resource officers to understand the complexities and vulnerabilities of the children of immigrants. As recommended by many, school resource officers should be entering schools with specialized training that does not regard children and youth in terms of crime or social control but rather centers community engagement, conflict resolution, mentoring, and education (Addington, 2009; May, 2014; Muschert & Peguero, 2010; Muschert, Henry, Bracy, & Peguero, 2013). Fourth, as noted in this book, immigrant parents often face cultural and language barriers when communicating with school administrators. This can be problematic for school sanctions because discussing school expulsion and suspension typically requires contacting students' parents. Faculty, staff, administrators, and security personnel should be thoughtful of the barriers that immigrant parents face when communicating with school personnel, as well as the potential fear of a law enforcement presence at the school.

5.3 School-Wide Positive Behavioral Interventions and Supports

School-Wide Positive Behavioral Interventions and Supports (SWP-BIS) is a comprehensive and proactive approach to behavior management in schools (Bradshaw, 2013; Bradshaw et al., 2012; Horner & Sugai, 2015; Ross, Romer, & Horner, 2012). SWPBIS is being widely disseminated by the U.S. Department of Education and several state departments of education. It is estimated that more than 9,000 schools across the United States have implemented this safety policy (Horner & Sugai, 2015). SWPBIS is based on the assumption that actively teaching and acknowledging teacher, school, and behavioral expectations can change the extent to which students expect appropriate behavior from themselves and each other (Bradshaw, 2013; Bradshaw, Waasdorp, & Leaf, 2012; Ross et al., 2012; Horner & Sugai,

2015). SWPBIS is a universal prevention strategy that aims to alter the school environment by creating improved systems that promote positive change in staff behaviors, which subsequently alter student behaviors. SWPBIS draws on behavioral, social learning, and organizational behavioral principles, which were traditionally used with individual students but have been generalized and applied to an entire student body consistently across all school settings (Bradshaw, 2013; Bradshaw et al., 2012; Ross et al., 2012; Horner & Sugai, 2015). When consistent, positive expectations are established by all adults in a school, evidence clearly exists that confirms that the proportion of students with serious behavior problems will be reduced and the school's overall social climate will improve.

The procedures that define SWPBIS are organized around three main themes: 1) prevention, 2) multi-tiered support, and 3) data-based decision making (Bradshaw, 2013; Bradshaw et al., 2012; Ross et al., 2012; Horner & Sugai, 2015). Investing in the prevention of problem behavior involves 1) defining and teaching a set of positively stated behavioral expectations to students, teachers, and parents (e.g., be safe, respectful, responsible); 2) acknowledging and rewarding those behaviors (e.g., compliance to school rules, safe and respectful peer-to-peer interactions, and academic effort/engagement); 3) systematically supervising students in classrooms and common areas; and 4) establishing and implementing a consistent continuum of corrective consequences for problem behavior. Schools are encouraged to reduce the use of out-of-class referrals and out-of-school suspensions as a response to problem behavior (Bradshaw, 2013; Bradshaw et al., 2012; Ross et al., 2012; Horner & Sugai, 2015). The goal is to establish a positive social climate in which behavioral expectations for students are directly taught, consistently acknowledged, and actively monitored.

There are three recommendations associated with immigration that should be considered by schools that incorporate SWPBIS practices. First, research suggests that different SWPBIS effects might be observed in schools that are resistant to adopting the model (Bradshaw, 2013; Bradshaw et al., 2012). As noted, the children of immigrants typically attend poorer schools with higher teacher and administrator turnover; therefore, predominantly immigrant, racial, and ethnic minority and urban schools face the serious challenge of not having the resources to successfully implement SWPBIS. Second, on a related note, SWPBIS training and sustainability for faculty, staff, and security personnel are vital for program success. Third, implementing school safety practices and rules that are believed to be fair and just by their students is fundamental; however, there is evidence that the children of immigrants' belief that their schools are fair and just diminishes as they assimilate (Bondy et al., 2019; Peguero, 2012a; Peguero & Bondy, 2015). Thus, schools that incorporate SWPBIS should be mindful of the educational inequities the children of immigrants endure in their daily experiences.

5.4 Communal Schools

Payne and colleagues (Gottfredson, 2001; Payne, 2008, 2016; Payne, Gottfredson, & Gottfredson, 2003) suggest that creating a strong communal school organization is an effective and efficient approach to providing a safe and healthy school climate for students. Defined as the organization of a school as a community, key characteristics include supportive relationships among teachers, administrators, and students, all of whom share a common set of goals and norms, collaboration, and involvement (Gottfredson, 2001; Payne, 2008, 2016; Payne et al., 2003). A strong communal school organization is found to reduce disorder, violence, and bullying, as well as increase academic interest, motivation, and achievement (Gottfredson, 2001; Payne, 2008, 2016; Payne et al., 2003). "Healthy" relationships between school administrators, teachers, and students positively influence the climate and effectiveness of that school (Gottfredson, 2001; Payne, 2008, 2016; Payne et al., 2003). Schools that implement programs that promote social issues awareness can yield positive results, such as increased school attachment, bonding, attendance, and engagement among all members of the school community (Gottfredson, 2001; Payne, 2008, 2016; Payne et al., 2003). School administrators, faculty, and staff who focus on establishing a learning climate that strives for academic excellence often positively influence the school's cultural attitude toward learning. That pursuit of academic excellence is argued to be "contagious" among students, teachers, and administrators in schools that promote such scholastic virtue (Gottfredson, 2001; Payne, 2008, 2016; Payne et al., 2003). The relationships between the school administrators, teachers, staff, and students directly and indirectly promote learning and safety. Policies and programs that focus on promoting the importance of educational achievement, attainment, and success improve the overall school climate, as well as making it safer.

Although there is evidence that communal schools can be effective in ameliorating violence, as well as improving safety, school administrators face a number of barriers in establishing communal schools in poor and urban areas, which typically have higher populations of immigrants. Even though strong student-teacher relationships, extracurricular activities, and effective collaborations between administrators and faculty can be identified as key elements for communal schools, the resources available to create and sustain a communal school are not always available. High administrator and teacher turnover, limited extracurricular activities, large classrooms, disorder, and low student expectations are historically and persistently evident within poor urban schools (Buchmann, Condron, & Roscigno, 2010; Lewis & Diamond, 2015; Morris, 2016; Noguera, 2009; Rios, 2011, 2017, Shedd, 2015). Although in an ideal sense, communal schools can be foundational to healthy, safe, and effective learning environments, there are structural barriers and inequalities that restrict stakeholders from attaining a communal school, particularly in poor communities.

There are three recommendations associated with immigration that should be considered by communal schools. First, communal school initiatives should focus on cultural awareness and sensitivity among students. This may be a fruitful avenue for improving school-based safety and fostering the social integration of the children of immigrants. More specifically, programs that promote open communication among peers and parents of linguistically and culturally diverse backgrounds, as well as extracurricular activities designed to combat intolerance, have been found to be effective at building culturally competent schools (Gottfredson, 2001; Payne, 2008, 2016; Payne et al., 2003). Second, communal school initiatives designed to promote prosocial behavior and student safety must give careful consideration to the changing demographic profile of today's elementary and secondary school populations and the unique challenges faced by immigrant youth. For example, the children of immigrants with limited English proficiency are more likely to report victimization, as well as feelings of being unsafe, while in school (Peguero, 2008, 2009, 2013). Research suggests that programs aimed at rapid English language acquisition, such as those outlined in Title III of the No Child Left Behind Act, may improve peer relationships, as well as facilitate violence and victimization reporting. Third, participation in academic and sports extracurricular activities is often encouraged by school faculty, counselors, and administrators to ameliorate persistent educational inequalities experienced by the children of immigrants and provide opportunities for success (Kao, Vaquera, & Goyette, 2013; Olsen, 2008; Rong & Preissle, 2008; Suárez-Orozco et al., 2009). As noted in this book, however, it appears that providing valuable opportunities, such as academic and sport extracurricular activities, may be a risk factor for violence and victimization against the children of immigrants that could negate any educational benefits gained from participation. It is important to emphasize that we are not recommending that extracurricular activity involvement should be discouraged. On the contrary, involvement in extracurricular activities has been consistently found to have many educational benefits. Administrators and educational policymakers should still consider the situational context of students who are involved in these beneficial activities, such as in bands, orchestras, academic clubs, plays, and student government, while considering school policies that attempt to ameliorate students' exposure to school violence and victimization. If a communal school approach intentionally promotes and advocates participation in academic and sport extracurricular activities as a way to promote or facilitate educational success, the overarching reality of the prevalence of discrimination and educational inequality within the school system must be addressed. Although these initiatives provide a solid footing from which to build more communal schools, there remains a critical dearth of research on the ways in which American schools are being reshaped by the new immigration.

5.5 Olweus Bullying Prevention Program

The Olweus bullying prevention program (OBPP) is a school-based program designed to prevent or reduce school bullying by identifying and focusing on three aspects of the school experience: 1) schoolwide, 2) classroom, and 3) the individual. At the *school level*, the first step of the program is to identify bullies and bullying victims (Espelage & Swearer, 2010; Olweus, Limber, & Mihalic, 1999). School faculty and staff administer the OBPP questionnaire to students in order to assess the prevalence and characteristics of bullying occurring among the student body (Espelage & Swearer, 2010; Olweus et al., 1999). Then school staff establishes a committee to implement training for all faculty and staff members in order to address bullying. Finally, faculty and staff develop curricula for all students that highlight the school-wide rules against bullying while promoting the importance of mutual respect and healthy relations among students. Within the *classroom*, teachers deliver a number of anti-bullying lessons or oversee student meetings about school bullying and peer relations (Espelage & Swearer, 2010; Olweus et al., 1999). Teachers also extend communication and discussions about school bullying with parents. At the *individual level*, students may be individually identified as a bully or bullying victim in order to have regularly scheduled meetings to discuss and address why the bullying is occurring and what can be done to resolve the violence. Via these mechanisms, the OBPP attempts to reorganize the school to decrease the occurrence of bullying.

Although the OBPP is generally viewed by school administrators as successful, there have been limited studies that examine the effectiveness and the limitations of anti-bullying programs, and inconsistent findings in these studies are common (see, e.g., Espelage, 2013; Hong, 2009; Osher et al., 2016; Peguero, 2012b). Because the definition of bullying is complex and relative (Espelage, 2013; Hong, 2009; Osher et al., 2016; Peguero, 2012b), the OBPP may not address all forms of perceived bullying. In this context, the perception of violence, injury, and victimization is primarily based on adult definitions and understandings of bullying, which may lead to under- or overmonitoring of violent student behavior (Espelage, 2013; Hong, 2009; Osher et al., 2016; Peguero, 2012b). In other words, interpretations by school administrators, faculty, and staff may influence the utilization of bullying prevention policies. Intimidation based on race, ethnicity, gender, religion, socioeconomic status, social class, physical ability, and sexual orientation are sometimes excluded from definitions of bullying and are therefore not addressed by anti-bullying policies (Espelage, 2013; Hong, 2009; Osher et al., 2016; Peguero, 2012b). Of course, this may be complicated by the relative and subjective definitions of each student, teacher, administrator, and parent's view of bullying.

There are three recommendations associated with immigration that should be considered by schools that incorporate OBPP practices. First, for OBPP to be successful, administrators and teachers must be trained to understand and identify behavioral problems and detrimental treatment in their classrooms; however, the children of immigrants are more likely to attend poor schools that are consequently less likely to have well-qualified teachers who could properly address the problems of bullying (Bondy, 2015; Hong, 2009; Kao et al., 2013; Peguero & Bondy, 2015). Second, as noted in this book, the children of immigrants are more likely to attend schools with increased levels of disorder, violence, and crime. Therefore, community disorder, violence, and crime may impose serious limitations to the effectiveness of OBPP practices because bullying is often constructed as comparatively "minor" and not pressing in such schools (Hong, 2009; Kao et al., 2013; Peguero & Bondy, 2015). Third, cultural disparities may pose a hurdle for OBPP practices. As discussed, because inconsistent definitions of school bullying exist, the complexities associated with misinterpreted interpersonal behaviors are embedded with social and cultural understandings (Bondy et al., 2015; Hong, 2009; Kao et al., 2013; Peguero & Bondy, 2015). Thus, OBPP facilitators should consider and be knowledgeable of the social and cultural distinctions associated with defining and responding to school bullying.

5.6 Restorative Justice in Schools

Originally applied within the criminal justice system, *restorative justice* interventions have attempted to repair the harm caused by criminal offenses while preventing further violence and crime; this is generally accomplished through mediation and conferences that reconcile conflicts between offenders, victims, and community members (González, 2012; Morrison & Vaandering, 2012; Pavelka, 2013). The importance of communication between offenders, victims, and the community affected by the violence is perceived as a resolution that facilitates closure for the victim and responsibility taken by the offender (González, 2012; Morrison & Vaandering, 2012; Pavelka, 2013). Allowing the offender to emphasize, discuss, and take accountability for the violent or harmful act is an important aspect of the restorative justice process and can minimize the reoccurrence of such behavior (González, 2012; Morrison & Vaandering, 2012; Pavelka, 2013). Communication between the victim and offender allows the offender to see how violence harms others and enables all of those impacted by the violent act to make a collaborative decision toward addressing the injury (González, 2012; Morrison & Vaandering, 2012; Pavelka, 2013). Restorative justice practices are gaining attention and utilization within schools as an alternative to stringent school punishment practices (González, 2012; Morrison & Vaandering, 2012; Pavelka, 2013).

Instead of excluding and punishing, restorative justice in schools treats violence as a form of conflict and thus acts proactively to find alternative ways to handle conflict, including peer mediation, or other forms of settlement-directed talking, such as restorative conferencing and peacemaking circles (González, 2012; Morrison & Vaandering, 2012; Pavelka, 2013; Payne & Welch, 2015). Completely contrary to the disciplinary practice of student exclusion, restorative approaches in schools focus on relationships, shifting from punishment and isolation to reconciliation and community (González, 2012; Morrison & Vaandering, 2012; Pavelka, 2013; Payne & Welch, 2015). Some argue that restorative justice is best applied to the school context because of the nature of relationships where students see each other day after day and encounters can turn dangerous if not adequately managed (González, 2012; Morrison & Vaandering, 2012; Pavelka, 2013; Payne & Welch, 2015). Within a restorative justice perspective, misbehavior is viewed as a violation of the relationship between teachers, administrators, and/ or other students (González, 2012; Morrison & Vaandering, 2012; Pavelka, 2013; Payne & Welch, 2015). In order to restore the harm of such a violation, the offending student and the individual whose trust was violated must reconcile, and the relationship must be mended. The importance of building and maintaining positive relationships, especially between members of a school community, is continually stressed (González, 2012; Morrison & Vaandering, 2012; Pavelka, 2013; Payne & Welch, 2015). Primary restorative practices involve the entire school community and aim at establishing common values, as well as skill bases for developing relational ecologies and resolving differences in respectful and caring ways. Secondary restorative practices address specific behaviors that disrupt the harmony and social relations of classrooms (e.g., problem-solving circles), hallways (e.g., corridor conferences), and playgrounds (e.g., peer mediations). Restorative practices are the most intensive, often responding to serious harm, and involve all those affected (including families, professionals, fellow students, and others affected) in a face-to-face restorative justice process (Morrison & Vaandering, 2012).

There are three recommendations associated with immigration that should be considered by schools that utilize restorative justice practices. First, because restorative justice often includes community stakeholders (for example, family members), school administrators should be mindful of the community's attitudes and beliefs about immigration. As noted in this book, it is plausible that the "threat of immigration" could be reflective of common community attitudes and parents' beliefs, and those may be transmitted through youth aggression. Second, because communication and empathy are essential to successful restorative justice practices between all parties involved, language barriers and cultural misunderstandings may impede the restorative justice process. Third, school administrators and teachers should be mindful of the potential tensions between immigrant and native-born students. Researchers have revealed that within pan-ethnic racial and ethnic groups (i.e., Asian American and Latina/o American), youth sustain tensions or conflict between immigrant and native-born (Hong et al., 2014, 2015; Lee, 2005, 2009; Lee & Zhou, 2015; Peguero, 2008, 2009). School administrators and faculty should learn the nuances and complexities associated with the vulnerabilities that immigrant youth face at school.

5.7 Considering Educational Success, Progress, and Well-Being With Safety

Any pursuit of ameliorating violence and ensuring the safety of the children of immigrants within school must also ensure the educational success and progress of this vulnerable student population. Historical and contemporary research examines the ongoing uneasiness between immigration and its influence on U.S. public education (Apple & Franklin, 2004; Kao et al., 2013; Rong & Preissle, 2008; Suárez-Orozco et al., 2009). Although these studies describe the role of schools in preserving and reproducing cultural, social, and economic inequalities, they have not sufficiently accounted for the role of school safety in perpetuating and/or disrupting such inequities. Schools are potentially a stage in the process of assimilation and incorporation in the United States, and the children of immigrants' experiences with school safety facilitate this process, increasing the odds of maintaining the already existing status quo. If schools are charged with being safe havens that nurture the potential for all youth to shape the nation and world, then understanding the children of immigrants' experiences with school safety is imperative.

Educational progress and success, particularly within the context of Common Core standards, high-stakes testing, and English-only education, typically focus on teaching strategies and objectively measurable outcomes, such as test score achievement. However, this book suggests that research on the children of immigrants should be attentive to a variety of schooling experiences that culminate in progress and success beyond technical responses to schooling problems, grades, and test scores. Efforts to understand how the children of immigrants assimilate and are incorporated into U.S. society must acknowledge that it is a social process that occurs through a variety of institutions, including schools. It is also important to remember that assimilation and incorporation processes across gender, race, ethnicity, and documentation status have perhaps not unfolded in an even and gradual acceptance of U.S. values, ideals, and beliefs. Researchers who are seeking to better understand the schooling experiences of immigrant

youth might benefit from questioning assimilation and Americanization as processes that inevitably promote educational progress. Given
that immigrant youth have historically been marginalized within U.S.
schools (Apple & Franklin, 2004; Portes & Rumbaut, 2014; Rong &
Preissle, 2008; Suárez-Orozco et al., 2009), it appears that socialization, gender, race, and documentation status are germane to creating
democratic education for all students.

In this chapter, we highlighted how school safety approaches (i.e.,
zero-tolerance and control, school-wide positive behavioral interventions and support, communal schools, Olweus bullying prevention
programs, and restorative justice) could benefit from including perspectives associated with immigration in order to pursue the children
of immigrants' safety and well-being while at school. Although we
discussed important factors associated with immigration for distinct
school safety approaches or programs, there are fundamental factors in
this context that warrant highlighting across school safety programs.
These are listed next.

First, language barriers and hurdles should be considered when
engaging the children of immigrants, as well as parents, guardians,
and/or extended family. It is often the case that extended family, such
as aunts and uncles, are advocates or guardians. Moreover, the children
of immigrants are often translators for their parents, guardians, and/or
extended family. Effective communication matters for safety program
success.

Second, the children of immigrants are subjugated to threats of
deportation from native-born peers, as well as faculty or security
personnel. Even though the children of immigrants are often U.S.
citizens, the reality of mixed immigration status families makes the
children of immigrants concerned and fearful of the deportation of
family members. These fears should be considered and acknowledged
when there is an increasing presence of law enforcement at schools.

Third, the social, cultural, and political debate about immigration
policy is heated and controversial. Unfortunately, the unintended consequences may make the children of immigrants vulnerable to harassment and victimization from faculty and administrators who are
responsible for the safety of all students, including the children of immigrants. School safety program leaders should be mindful of such biases.

Fourth, because schools are a site of socialization and Americanization for the children of immigrants, the effect of school violence and
victimization, as well as punishment and discipline, could have derailing effects on this marginalized and vulnerable youth population.

Fifth, the hurdles and barriers that the children of immigrants face at school in terms of their safety and learning also intersect with the inequities linked to race and ethnicity, region of origin, religion, gender, sexual orientation, language proficiency, and socioeconomic status. The identities that the children of immigrants encapsulate are dynamic and complex. School safety program leaders should be mindful not to stereotype or homogenize the children of immigrants and consider the myriad vulnerabilities that the children of immigrants endure at school.

References

Addington, L. A. (2009). Cops & cameras: Public school security as a policy response to Columbine. *American Behavioral Scientist, 52*(10), 1426–1446.

American Psychological Association. (2012). *Crossroads: The psychology of immigration in the new century.* Washington, DC: American Psychological Association.

Apple, M., & Franklin, B. (2004). Curricular history and social control. In M. Apple (Ed.), *Ideology and curriculum* (pp. 59–76). New York: Routledge Falmer.

Boler, M., & Zembylas, M. (2003). Discomforting truths: The emotional terrain of understanding difference. In P. P. Trifonas (Ed.), *Pedagogies of difference: Rethinking education for social change* (pp. 103–136). New York: Routledge Falmer.

Bondy, J. M. (2015). Hybrid citizenship: Latina youth and the politics of belonging. *The High School Journal, 98*(4), 353–373.

Bondy, J. M., Peguero, A. A., & Johnson, B. E. (2019). The children of immigrants' bonding to school: Examining the roles of assimilation, gender, race, ethnicity, and social bonds. *Urban Education, 54*, 592–622.

Bradshaw, C. P. (2013). Preventing bullying through positive behavioral interventions and supports (PBIS): A multi-tiered approach to prevention and integration. *Theory into Practice, 52*, 288–295.

Bradshaw, C. P., Waasdorp, T. E., & Leaf, P. J. (2012). Effects of school-wide positive behavioral interventions and supports on child behavior problems. *Pediatrics, 130*(5), e1136–e1145.

Buchmann, C., Condron, D., & Roscigno, V. (2010). Shadow education, American style: Test preparation, the SAT and college enrollment. *Social Forces, 89*, 435–462.

Crenshaw, K., Ocen, P., & Nanda, J. (2015). *Black girls matter: Pushed out, over-policed, and underprotected.* New York: Center for Intersectionality and Social Policy Studies, Columbia University.

Espelage, D. L. (2013). Why are bully prevention programs failing in US schools? *Journal of Curriculum and Pedagogy, 10*(2), 121–124.

Espelage, D. L., & Swearer, S. M. (2010). *Bullying in North American schools.* New York: Routledge Falmer.

Foucault, M. (1977). *Discipline and punish: The birth of the prison.* New York: Vintage Books.

Gonzales, R. G. (2016). *Lives in limbo: Undocumented and coming of age in America.* Berkeley, CA: University of California Press.

González, T. (2012). Keeping kids in schools: Restorative justice, punitive discipline, and the school to prison pipeline. *Journal of Law & Education, 41*(2), 281–335.

Gottfredson, D. C. (2001). *Schools and delinquency.* New York: Cambridge University Press.

Gregory, A., Skiba, R. J., & Noguera, P. A. (2010). The achievement gap and the discipline gap: Two sides of the same coin? *Educational Researcher, 39*(1), 59–68.

Hong, J. S. (2009). Feasibility of the Olweus bullying prevention program in low-income schools. *Journal of School Violence, 8*, 81–97.

Hong, J. S., Merrin, G. J., Crosby, S., Jozefowicz, D. M., Lee, J. M., & Allen-Meares, P. (2015). Individual and contextual factors associated with immigrant youth feeling unsafe in school: A social-ecological analysis. *Journal of Immigrant and Minority Health*, 1–11.

Hong, J. S., Peguero, A. A., Choi, S., Lanesskog, D., Espelage, D., & Lee, N. Y. (2014). School bullying and peer victimization of Latino and Asian American youth: A social-ecological framework. *Journal of School Violence, 13*, 315–338.

Horner, R. H., & Sugai, G. (2015). School-wide PBIS: An example of applied behavior analysis implemented at a scale of social importance. *Behavior Analysis in Practice, 8*(1), 80–85.

Kao, G., Vaquera, E., & Goyette, K. (2013). *Education and immigration.* Malden, MA: Policy Press.

Kim, C. Y., Losen, D. J., & Hewitt, D. T. (2010). *The school-to-prison pipeline: Structuring legal reform.* New York: New York University Press.

Kupchik, A. (2010). *Homeroom security: School discipline in an age of fear.* New York: New York University Press.

Kupchik, A. (2016). *The real school safety problem: The long-term consequences of harsh school punishment.* Oakland: University of California Press.

Lee, S. J. (2005). *Up against Whiteness: Race, school and immigrant youth.* New York: Teachers College Press.

Lee, S. J. (2009). *Unraveling the model minority stereotype: Listening to Asian American youth.* New York: Teachers College Press.

Lee, S. J., & Zhou, M. (2015). *The Asian American achievement paradox.* New York: Russell Sage Foundation.

Lewis, A. E., & Diamond, J. B. (2015). *Despite the best intentions: How racial inequality thrives in good schools.* Oxford: Oxford University Press.

May, D. C. (2014). *School safety in America: A reasoned look at the rhetoric.* New York: Carolina Academic Press.

Morris, M. W. (2016). *Pushout: The criminalization of Black girls in schools.* New York: The New Press.

Morrison, B. E., & Vaandering, D. (2012). Restorative justice: Pedagogy, praxis, and discipline. *Journal of School Violence, 11*(2), 138–155.

Muschert, G. W., Henry, S., Bracy, N. L., & Peguero, A. A. (2013). *Responses to school violence: Confronting the Columbine effect.* Boulder, CO: Lynne Reinner Publishers.

Muschert, G. W., & Peguero, A. A. (2010). The Columbine effect and school anti-violence policy. *Research in Social Problems & Public Policy, 17,* 117–148.

Noguera, P. A. (2009). *The trouble with Black boys: And other reflections on race, equity, and the future of public education.* San Francisco, CA: Jossey-Bass.

Olsen, L. (2008). *Made in America: Immigrant students in our public schools.* New York: New York University Press.

Olweus, D., Limber, S., & Mihalic, S. (1999). *Bullying prevention program: Blueprints for violence prevention.* Boulder, CO: Center for the Study and Prevention of Violence.

Osher, D., Kidron, Y., Brackett, M., Dymnicki, A., Jones, S., & Weissberg, R. P. (2016). Advancing the science and practice of social and emotional learning: Looking back and moving forward. *Review of Research in Education, 40*(1), 644–681.

Pavelka, S. (2013). Practices and policies for implementing restorative justice within schools. *The Prevention Researcher, 20*(1), 15–18.

Payne, A. A. (2008). A multilevel model of the relationships among communal school disorder, student bonding, and delinquency. *Journal of Research in Crime and Delinquency, 45,* 429–455.

Payne, A. A. (2016). *Creating and sustaining a positive and communal school climate: Contemporary research, present obstacles, and future directions.* Retrieved from www.ncjrs.gov/pdffiles1/nij/250209.pdf

Payne, A. A., Gottfredson, D. C., & Gottfredson, G. D. (2003). Schools as communities: The relationships among communal school disorder, student bonding, and school disorder. *Criminology, 41,* 749–778.

Payne, A. A., & Welch, K. (2015). Restorative justice in schools: The influence of race on restorative discipline. *Youth & Society, 47*(4), 539–564.

Peguero, A. A. (2008). Is immigrant status relevant in school violence research? An analysis with Latino students. *Journal of School Health, 78,* 397–404.

Peguero, A. A. (2009). Victimizing the children of immigrants: Latino and Asian American student victimization. *Youth & Society, 41,* 186–208.

Peguero, A. A. (2012a). The children of immigrants' diminishing perceptions of just and fair punishment. *Punishment & Society, 14,* 429–451.

Peguero, A. A. (2012b). Schools, bullying, and inequality: Intersecting factors and complexities with the stratification of youth victimization at school. *Sociology Compass, 6,* 402–412.

Peguero, A. A. (2013). An adolescent victimization immigrant paradox?: School-based routines, lifestyles, and victimization across immigration generations. *Journal of Youth and Adolescence, 42,* 1759–1773.

Peguero, A. A., & Bondy, J. M. (2015). Schools, justice, and immigrant students: Assimilation, race, ethnicity, gender, and perceptions of fairness and order. *Teachers College Record, 117,* 1–42.

Peguero, A. A., & Hong, J. S. (2019). Are violence and disorder at school placing adolescents within immigrant families at higher risk of dropping out? *Journal of School Violence, 18*(2), 241–258.

Peguero, A. A., Shekarkhar, Z., Popp, A. M., & Koo, D. J. (2015). Punishing the children of immigrants: Race, ethnicity, generational status, and student misbehavior and school discipline. *Journal of Immigrant & Refugee Studies: Special Issue, Immigration and Civil Society, 13*(2), 200–220.

Portes, A., & Rumbaut, R. (2014). *Immigrant America: A portrait.* Berkeley, CA: University of California Press.

Portillos, E., González, J. C., & Peguero, A. A. (2012). Crime control strategies in school: Chicanos/as perceptions and criminalization. *The Urban Review, 44*(2), 171–188.

Rios, V. M. (2011). *Punished: Policing the lives of Black and Latino boys.* New York: New York University Press.

Rios, V. M. (2017). *Human targets: Schools, police, and the criminalization of Latino youth.* Chicago, IL: The University of Chicago Press.

Rong, X., & Preissle, J. (2008). *Educating immigrant students in the 21st century: What we need to know to meet the challenges.* Thousand Oaks, CA: Corwin Press.

Ross, S. W., Romer, N., & Horner, R. H. (2012). Teacher well-being and the implementation of school-wide positive behavior interventions and supports. *Journal of Positive Behavior Interventions, 14*(2), 118–128.

Shedd, C. (2015). *Unequal city: Race, schools, and perceptions of injustice.* New York: Russell Sage Foundation.

Simon, J. (2010). *Governing through crime: How the war on crime transformed American democracy and created a culture of fear.* New York: Oxford University Press.

Skiba, R. J., Horner, R. H., Chung, C. G., & Rausch, M. K. (2011). Race is not neutral: A national investigation of African American and Latino disproportionality in school discipline. *School Psychology Review, 40,* 85–107.

Stevens, L. P., & Stovall, D. O. (2011). Critical literacy for xenophobia: A wake-up call. *Journal of Adult and Adolescent Literacy, 54,* 295–298.

Suárez-Orozco, C., Suárez-Orozco, M., & Todorova, I. (2009). *Learning a new land: Immigrant students in American society.* Cambridge, MA: Harvard University Press.

United States Census Bureau. (2017). *Current population survey.* Washington, DC: United States Census Bureau, Population Division.

Young, I. M. (2011). *Justice and the politics of difference.* Princeton, NJ: Princeton University Press.

Zembylas, M. (2010). Teachers' emotional experiences of growing diversity and multiculturalism in schools and the prospects of an ethic of discomfort. *Teachers and Teaching: Theory into Practice, 16*(6), 703–716.

Zembylas, M. (2012). Transnationalism, migration and emotions: Implications for education. *Globalisation, Societies and Education, 10,* 163–179.

Chapter 6

Conclusion

At the Current Historical Moment

As we are completing this book for submission, we would like to acknowledge the current historical moment by discussing three significant sociocultural events directly connected to our book about immigration and school safety: 1) COVID-19, 2) the Black Lives Matter movement, and 3) the 2020 Supreme Court ruling on DACA. This section will provide a brief discussion about how this current historical moment could mark a turning point that highlights the need to address the vulnerabilities that the children of immigrants endure daily in communities and schools.

There are three overarching factors in thinking about how COVID-19 is relevant to this topic of immigration and school safety: 1) the U.S. justice system, 2) education, and 3) hate crime. Miller and colleagues (2020) provide a broad overview of how COVID-19 is influencing the relationship between immigration and the U.S. justice system. In essence, they argue that the vulnerabilities and inequalities immigrants and their children faced prior to COVID-19 are only being exacerbated. Concerns have been raised about aggressive policy changes, enforcement actions, immigrant detention, and deportation practices in response to and during the COVID-19 outbreak (Miller, Ripepi, Ernstes, & Peguero, 2020). All of these actions are having detrimental consequences on immigrants and their children in regard to their safety, health, and overall well-being. Second, Viner and colleagues (2020) offer a broad overview of how COVID-19 is influencing educational systems in the United States and globally. They describe how schools have basically been shut down. At this moment, it remains unknown when and how public schools will even reopen. It is easy to predict that how we understand "school safety" in regard to violence and crime will now include conceptualizations of public health and well-being for the entire school community in a post-COVID-19 era. Third, Tessler and colleagues (2020) offer a broad overview of how COVID-19 is exacerbating Asian American vulnerabilities associated with hate crimes and negative biases. It is evident that COVID-19 has elevated the risks of Asian Americans to hate crimes and business vandalism. Asian Americans have historically been viewed as perpetually foreign, no matter how long they have lived in the United States. It is, therefore, argued that present-day sociocultural beliefs constructing Asian Americans as foreign and diseased are historical and persistent (Tessler et al., 2020). The hate crimes and negative biases against Asian Americans in the time of COVID-19 highlight how additional burdens of anxiety, economic instability, and risk of violence and victimization are imposed upon Asian Americans. Of course, understandings of school safety and how we pursue such understandings in a post-COVID-19 context remain unknown, especially in regard to the implications for the children of immigrants.

The social and cultural protests around the recent tragic deaths of George Floyd, Breonna Taylor, and Ahmaud Arbery and the calls for racial justice have been magnified through civil unrest throughout the United States and world. Such protests have centered around the Black Lives Matter movement. Taylor (2016) offers a broad overview of the Black Lives Matter movement; however, the civil unrest and protests within the United States have re-centered historical and systemic social problems of racial inequality and oppression within the criminal justice system, including the growing presence of law enforcement in schools. As noted throughout this book, the disproportionate surveillance, punishment, discriminatory treatment, and inequitable access to educational resources for racial/ethnic minority students are historical and persistent, with detrimental consequences for the children of immigrants. Social, public, and media discourses about defunding law enforcement and terminating the utilization of school resource officers across U.S. schools have emerged from the protests about racial inequity within the criminal justice system. Without a doubt, if law enforcement is defunded and police and school resource officers' presence within schools is ended, this would have profound, fundamental, and unclear implications for school safety overall, especially for racial/ethnic minorities and the children of immigrants.

In June 2020, the Supreme Court blocked the Trump administration's attempt to end DACA, citing efforts to end the program as "arbitrary and capricious." DACA beneficiaries breathed a sigh of relief as the

Supreme Court decision allowed them to continue to stay in school, at work, and remain with relatives while being protected from deportation. However, the Supreme Court decision also paved the way for the Trump administration to try and end DACA once again, as long as they follow the appropriate process. With the election of Biden as the next president of the United States, it is highly probable that pursuits to end DACA in the next four years will cease, particularly given bipartisan support for the program. Undocumented students will nevertheless be left with uncertain futures. Without a clear path to permanent residency and citizenship, and without comprehensive immigration reform, undocumented students and families will not be able to rest easily. As the United States edges closer to its next presidential administration, it will be important to explore the school safety implications of DACA and potential pathways to citizenship for the children of immigrants.

We have noted throughout this book that social, cultural, and political contexts frame how we understand the associations between immigration, education, and safety in our nation. It is uncertain if and how COVID-19, the Black Lives Matter movement, and the 2020 Supreme Court ruling on DACA will influence the evident vulnerabilities that the children of immigrants endure daily in communities and schools. Nevertheless, we have a duty and responsibility to highlight these historic events in regard to immigration and school safety.

Overall Summary

This book sought to highlight how the subject of immigration matters to our nation's pursuits of addressing school violence and ensuring safe learning environments for all youth. The research presented in this book reveals that important advances to the field can be achieved by attempting to better understand the correlates, contexts, and consequences of immigration in association with school violence and safety, educational progress and success, and juvenile justice. We will summarize the highlights of each chapter in this book.

In the second chapter titled "How Immigration Matters With School Violence and Safety," we discussed how the context of reception for immigrants and their children contributed to the vulnerability of violence and victimization. We also highlighted the complexities and details surrounding the "immigrant criminal" myth, as well as how it mattered for the safety of immigrants and their children. We explained that the detrimental treatment and disproportionate punishment of the children of immigrants can be associated with a school to prison/deportation pipeline. We also described how the heated and controversial social, political, and educational debate over immigration could be establishing barriers and hurdles for ensuring the safety and well-being of immigrants and their children. We explained three different theories of assimilation, such as straight-line, segmented, and immigrant optimism hypotheses, and their relevance to school safety, as well as educational progress.

In the third chapter titled "Intersecting Factors Associated With Immigration and Safety," we provided research that demonstrated how the exposure of violence and victimization at school are disparate across distinct segments of the student population, especially for the children of immigrants. We presented evidence that the population of children of immigrants attending U.S. schools is diverse, with distinct experiences involving violence and safety. We reviewed and empha-sized the importance of understanding the intersection of factors such as race, ethnicity, region of origin, gender, English language profi-ciency, family, and documentation status in order to address school violence and ensure school safety for the children of immigrants.

In the fourth chapter titled "The Significance of Criminology The-ories," we explained the importance of including criminology theo-ries (i.e., social-ecology, social bonds, opportunity, minority threat, and procedural justice) in analyzing factors affecting the children of immigrants' safety and well-being while at school. The "one-size-fits-all" or a "standardized" approach toward making schools safe may not be effective considering the distinct vulnerabilities that the children of immigrants face in the U.S. school system. Thus, we argued it is important for researchers to not only utilize criminology theories to understand the causes and correlates of school safety but also be mind-ful that the children of immigrants face unique challenges and com-plex realities with regard to school violence and safety. Without a doubt, utilizing criminology theories to address school violence and ensure safety for all youth is pressing; however, it is vital to also estab-lish the safety of youth who are marginalized and vulnerable due to being the children of immigrants.

In the fifth chapter titled "The Implications and Importance of Considering Immigration With School Safety," we highlighted how school safety programs and approaches could benefit from including factors associated with immigration in order to pursue the safety and well-being of children of immigrants while at school. We highlighted five important factors that matter across school safety programs. First, language barriers and hurdles should be considered when engag-ing the children of immigrants, as well as parents, guardians, and/or extended family. Second, even though the children of immigrants are often U.S. citizens, the reality of mixed immigration status families makes the children of immigrants concerned and fearful about the potential deportation of family members. Third, heated and controversial debate about immigration policy may be placing the children of immigrants at risk of harassment and victimization. Fourth, because schools are a site of socialization and Americanization for the children of immigrants, the effect of school violence and victimization, as well as punishment and discipline, could have derailing effects for this marginalized and vulnerable youth population. Fifth, the hurdles and barriers that the children of immigrants face at school in terms of their safety and learning also intersect with inequities linked to race and ethnicity, region of origin, religion, gender, sexual orientation, language proficiency, and socioeconomic status.

In conclusion, we encourage future research to further expand our understanding of school violence, safety, and juvenile justice for the children of immigrants. The growing numbers of students in immigrant families provide both a challenge and an opportunity for the United States, much as they did at the turn of the twentieth century. As these children grow and graduate from high school and college, enter the labor force, become voters, form families, and, ultimately, lead the United States into its future, research promises to provide important opportunities for theoretical advancement on racial/ethnic democracy, crime, and justice.

References

Miller, H. V., Ripepi, M., Ernstes, A. M., & Peguero, A. A. (2020). Immigration policy and justice in the era of COVID-19. *American Journal of Criminal Justice*, 1–17.

Taylor, K. Y. (2016). *From #BlackLivesMatter to Black liberation*. Chicago: Haymarket Books.

Tessler, H., Choi, M., & Kao, G. (2020). The anxiety of being Asian American: Hate crimes and negative biases during the COVID-19 pandemic. *American Journal of Criminal Justice*, 1–11.

Viner, R. M., Russell, S. J., Croker, H., Packer, J., Ward, J., Stansfield, C., . . . Booy, R. (2020). School closure and management practices during coronavirus outbreaks including COVID-19: A rapid systematic review. *The Lancet Child & Adolescent Health*, 4.

Index

For Product Safety Concerns and Information please contact our EU
representative GPSR@taylorandfrancis.com
Taylor & Francis Verlag GmbH, Kaufingerstraße 24, 80331 München, Germany

www.ingramcontent.com/pod-product-compliance
Lightning Source LLC
Chambersburg PA
CBHW050538270326
41926CB00015B/3290

9 780367 741181